THE ULTIMATE FORMULA 1 TRIVIA BOOK

THE F1 FAN'S GUIDE

TO MUST-KNOW TERMINOLOGY, LEGENDARY
DRIVERS, FAMOUS CIRCUITS, *and More*

BERNADETTE JOHNSON

ULYSSES PRESS

Published by:
Ulysses Press
PO Box 3440
Berkeley, CA 94703
www.ulyssespress.com

ISBN: 978-1-64604-738-3
Library of Congress Control Number: 2024934551

Printed in the United States
10 9 8 7 6 5 4 3 2 1

Acquisitions editor: Claire Seilaff
Managing editor: Claire Chun
Project editor: Yesenia Garcia-Lopez
Editor: Renee Rutledge
Proofreader: Mary Calvez
Front cover design: Akangksha Sarmah
Artwork: cover car FrankBoston/Adobe Stock; cover flag vegefox.com/
    Adobe Stock; interior flag © Patthana Nirangkul/shutterstock.com;
    folio car © Om Bing Collection/shutterstock.com

IMPORTANT NOTE TO READERS: Although the author and publisher have made every effort to ensure that the information in this book was correct at press time, the author and publisher do not assume and hereby disclaim any liability to any party for any loss, damage, or disruption caused by errors or omissions, whether such errors or omissions result from negligence, accident, or any other cause.

To Jeff and Molly, my F1 couch crew.

CONTENTS

INTRODUCTION

Many describe Formula 1 as the pinnacle of motorsports, and they aren't lying. F1's 73-year history is filled with amazing stories, incredible feats, and unforgettable moments—from awe inspiring to tragic—that have taken place all over the globe since its inception. It is literally a sport of blood, sweat, and tears—one that takes an enormous amount of work, talent, ingenuity, and lots and lots of money. This book is both a celebration and an illumination of all things Formula 1, from the earliest Grands Prix to the latest champions, from old circuits to new, and from the older and much simpler rules to the complex multibook regulations that define the sport today. These regulations are and always have been the *formula* that makes Formula 1 what it is and differentiates it from other motorsports, even its other single-seater opened-wheel relatives, some of which are stepping stones that train and feed new drivers into the ranks of F1.

In the pages to come, you'll follow teams all over the world as they race across the arid desert track of Bahrain, the glamorous streets of Monte Carlo, the scenic old European countryside, and the glitzy Las Vegas Strip, among many others. These days, over 20 Grand Prix weekends take place per season! Learn how sleek aerodynamic F1 cars harness the laws of physics to glue themselves to the road (and sometimes fly off of it) at speeds reaching, and sometimes exceeding, 200 miles per hour! And shudder at the power and speed of these cutting-edge modern marvels of automotive ingenuity.

Drivers vie for that coveted spot on the first-place podium, even sparking rivalries between teammates, but F1 is a team sport with a great many people behind the scenes that make it happen, including drivers, engineers, pit crews, team bosses, race managers, marketers, fitness trainers, chefs, and aerodynamicists. It takes thousands of people and millions, no, *billions*, of dollars to keep it all going. The questions and answers within cover as many aspects of the sport as possible, while still only scratching the surface.

You will read about the drivers and teams from yesteryear through today and the intoxicating highs and the tragic lows as well as the just plain weird and wonderful. Whether you're a lifelong fan or just getting started with Formula 1, you can now witness what so many spectators and participants have experienced over Formula 1's fascinating history. So strap in, rev your engines, and burn rubber through the ultimate Formula 1 trivia journey. Prepare to qualify.

CHAPTER 1

START YOUR ENGINES

F1 TERMINOLOGY

Q: What is the governing body of Formula 1 racing?

A: The Fédération Internationale de l'Automobile (FIA) sets the sporting and technical rules and guidelines for Formula 1 racing. These include the rules of the actual races, the technical specs of the vehicles and equipment, and the fiscal rules regarding the teams' finances and prize money. See Chapter 7 for more information about this decades-old institution that oversees more than just Formula 1 racing.

Q: What is a circuit?

A: A circuit is a racetrack. F1 circuits can be permanent tracks built for racing year round or temporary tracks on regular roads set up just during race weekends then broken back down.

Q: What is a Grand Prix?

A: A Grand Prix (GP), French for "big prize," is one of the individual weekend-long racing competitions that are part of the Formula 1 World Championship, the competition that Formula 1 teams compete in annually to determine the team and driver rankings each year. They are held at different circuits all over the world. The F1 Grand Prix lineup changes from year to year.

Q: What is the pit in racing?

A: The pit is an area where a team's driver pulls off the track for mid-race maintenance like changing the tires, making repairs to the vehicle, and, formerly, refueling (see Chapter 7 for why refueling at a pit stop was banned in Formula 1). Each team has its own pit. In the lead up to the pit, the driver pulls off the track onto a special lane called the pit lane. Pulling off into the pit is called "making a pit stop," a phrase that has leaked into the English language as having to stop and do something (often used to mean going to the bathroom).

Q. Why are the pits called "the pits"?

A. The pits on a racetrack used to involve actual pits, dug out where the crew would sit right at the side of the racetrack to wave signals to their drivers, dangerously close to the action. A pit wall that separates the various pit crews from the track was eventually implemented at all circuits and has been modified to further improve safety over the decades.

Q. What group of people man the pit stops?

A. The group of people who scramble to change tires and fix the car when a driver stops at the pit is called "the pit crew." See Chapter 9 for more on the different responsibilities of the pit crew.

Q. Where do the cars line up at the start of the race?

A. The cars line up two by two at the start of the race on what's called "the starting grid." The starting positions on the grid are marked off with white paint.

Q. Who was the lollipop man in an F1 team crew?

A. The lollipop man was a member of the pit crew who signaled the driver where to stop the car, when to shift into first gear, and when to take off from the pit once the pit crew had finished its work on the car. The lollipop man did this by holding up a carbon fiber rod with a flat round part on the end that had different signs on either side—one saying to brake and the other to shift into first. The apparatus was shaped somewhat like a lollipop, thus the name. The lollipop man held the sign out in front of the car where the driver could see it, first displaying the breaking sign, then flipping to the first gear sign when the pit stop was close to an end. When he lifted the "lollipop," it signaled the driver that they could zoom out of the pit and rejoin the race. The lollipop man and his (or her) handheld sign have been replaced by a traffic light operator, who, very like the lollipop man, observes everything going on at the pit stop and activates lights on an overhanging bar in front of the driver to signal to them what to do.

Q: What are marks in F1 pit lingo?

A: Marks are strips of tape put down in the pit by a team's pit crew to show the driver exactly where to stop in the pit. This allows the crew to keep their equipment where it needs to be to get the car up to speed with fresh replacement tires or otherwise maintained or fixed as quickly as possible, shaving valuable seconds off of each pit stop.

Q: What is downforce?

A: Downforce is the force that pushes the car down onto the track, generated by the car's aerodynamic design and how it reacts with the air. It is essentially the opposite of lift, which is what makes airplanes leave the ground.

Q: What is drag?

A: Drag is a concept in fluid dynamics that involves a force pushing in the opposite direction of the motion of an object moving through the fluid. Fluids include both liquids and gases, so drag applies to air pushing against, say, a race car moving through the air. In this case, drag is air resistance working against the car and slowing it down. It is something to be avoided or countered in F1, but is an integral part of racing, especially drag racing.

Q: What is a reserve driver?

A: A reserve driver is on the sidelines, so to speak, to take over if one of the two official team drivers can't race for any reason. The reserve driver has to take part in at least one practice session as well as qualifying during a race weekend in order to take the place of one of the main drivers in an actual Grand Prix race. The reserve driver rarely gets to participate in the actual race, but they tend to do a lot of work in the simulator and practice sessions to help make performance improvements to the vehicles in between races.

Q: What is a third driver?

A: A third driver, sometimes called a test driver, tests the vehicles, sometimes participates in practice runs on Grand Prix weekends, and is often the driver used during promotional activities.

Q: What is a pay driver?

A: A pay driver is a driver added to the team because of the money or resources they can contribute to the team. Some pay drivers have turned out to be highly talented.

Q: What is the leader of a Formula 1 team called?

A: The leader of an F1 team is called "the team principal," aka a team boss. The roles of the team bosses vary by team, but they tend to make decisions for the team involving all aspects of the sport (from commercial to technical to sporting), staffing key positions and running the show year-round from car construction to testing and practice to the goings-on on race weekends. See Chapter 9 for more on team bosses and their roles and responsibilities.

Q: What is hitting the apex?

A: The apex in racing is the point at an inside corner that would take the car the shortest distance through a corner. Hitting the apex is when a driver gets as close to the apex as possible on a turn, which ensures that the car drives as straight a line as possible, theoretically cutting down on the total race distance and time.

Q: What is the safety car?

A: The safety car is deployed on the track to slow the cars down in the event of an accident or other hazard.

Q: What is a chicane?

A: A chicane is a series of corners on the circuit that are close together and change direction at least twice. See Chapter 5 for their purpose.

Q: How many timing sectors are on a track during a race?

A: There are three timing sectors where the race car times are measured and compared to each other.

Q: What is a marshal in F1?

A: Marshals oversee safety of competitors and spectators alike during F1 races. They perform various tasks, including waving flags to warn drivers of track conditions and getting stranded cars off the track.

Q: What is a steward in F1?

A: Three stewards are appointed to make major decisions during each Grand Prix.

Q: What is a marshaling sector?

A: There are 20 marshaling sectors used by marshals, stewards, directors, and other racing officials to do things like display flags or signal the VSC on a digital display screen. Read on to find out more about the VSC.

Q: What is the VSC in F1?

A: The VSC is the virtual safety car. As the name implies, it is not an actual car, but when the marshaling stations and dash displays show the VSC is in effect, all the drivers have to slow down, usually to a speed that's around 30 percent slower than the typical lap time. The lap time they must maintain is displayed on the cars' steering wheels. The drivers have to hit a speed lower than the VSC-prescribed speed at least once in each marshaling sector and also must be behind the VSC speed when the race resumes to avoid being penalized. The drivers are given a warning of about 15 seconds before the VSC mode ends. This virtual safety car mode ensures that all cars are slowed to a safer speed but also that they don't lose their places when the race resumes at full speed.

e? What is the VSC delta time?

4? The virtual safety car delta time shows drivers where they are in relation to the virtual safety car prescribed lap time. The delta time shows the drivers how much faster or slower they are going than the VSC time and therefore gives them the info they need to keep pace by slowing down or speeding up. Delta positive means they are below the VSC lap time; delta negative means they are above the time; and delta zero means they are exactly keeping pace with the VSC time.

e? What is a backmarker?

4? A backmarker is a slower car on the track that is often passed by the leading cars.

e? What is ballast on an F1 car?

4? Ballast is weight added to the car to improve handling and to bring the car to the minimum weight required by the Formula 1 rules.

e? What is the frame of a race car called?

4? The main frame of an F1 race car, or any car, for that matter, is called a chassis.

e? What is a monocoque?

4? A monocoque is a chassis formed as a single piece of material rather than the old space-frame method of bolting multiple parts together to form a chassis. It is a central part of the modern F1 racecar that includes the driver cockpit.

Q: What is the area where the driver sits called in an F1 car?

A: The area where the driver sits is called the cockpit, just like the pilot's compartment of a plane.

Q: What is a lap?

A: A lap is one drive around the entire length of a given track from the starting line all the way back to the starting line. Read on to find out about special types of laps.

Q: What is the installation lap?

A: The installation lap is the first lap that a driver takes in the car during a pre-race practice session to make sure that their vehicle and equipment are in proper working order.

Q: What is a formation lap?

A: A formation lap (aka parade lap or warm-up lap) is a lap that the cars take before the start of the race to line up in their starting positions, or get in formation, so to speak.

Q: What is a Grand Slam in F1 racing?

A: A Grand Slam (aka Grand Chelem) is a perfect race where a driver wins from pole position, leads every lap, and sets the fastest lap. Only 25 drivers in F1 history have achieved this.

Q: What is a paddock in F1 racing?

A: A paddock is the area of the circuit behind each team's pit where their equipment lives and where their staff perform all their functions.

Q: What is the Parc fermé?

A: In French, parc means "park" and fermé means "closed." Parc fermé (or closed park) is the area of the paddock where the cars are kept under lock and key after qualifying and before the race. No one is allowed to tamper with them while they are in this location.

Q: What is the podium in F1?

A: As in many sports, the podium is a three-tiered platform where the top three finishers in a race stand to receive their trophies. If you hear that a driver "scored a podium," it means that they won one of these coveted spots.

Q: What is the pole position?

A: The pole position is the spot on the starting grid that is achieved by the driver who sets the fastest time in Q3 (the last of three qualifying periods). It is the front position.

Q: What are practice sessions in F1?

A: There are three one-hour-long practice sessions during an F1 race weekend, two on Friday and one on Saturday morning before the qualifying round begins. As the name implies, these allow drivers to practice driving and setting up the car for the race.

Q: What is the qualifying session in F1?

A: The qualifying session determines where the drivers will line up on the starting grid for the race, based on how each driver's fastest qualifying lap compares to all the other drivers' fastest laps. This session takes place on Saturday afternoon on an F1 Grand Prix weekend.

Q: What are the bits of rubber that F1 tires shed during races called?

A: The bits of tire that are inevitably shed when race cars corner at high speed are referred to as marbles.

Q: What is a constructor?

A: A constructor is a team. In Formula 1, each team constructs its own cars. In the case of teams that are owned by car companies (like Scuderia Ferrari, McLaren, and Mercedes), many of the parts are manufactured by the company. In the case of teams that are not run by car companies (like Haas and Red Bull Racing), the parts are purchased from others, often from their own F1 competitors.

Q: What is a power unit?

A: Power unit is the current term for the engine plus the other parts that give power to the car. When people speak of the engine of a Formula 1 car, they may be talking about either the internal combustion engine (ICE) or the whole power unit. See Chapter 4 for more details on this complex and expensive part of an F1 vehicle.

Q: What are the different categories of F1 teams?

A: There are several terms you might hear to describe categories of Formula 1 teams. The slate of teams has changed over the decades, so how many of each type of team changes, and some teams fit into more than one category. Here are the major team types:

- ⮑ Works teams (aka factory teams or manufacturer teams) are teams that are owned and operated by car manufacturers, who design their own power units used by their Formula 1 teams. Current factory teams include Scuderia Ferrari, Mercedes, and Alpine (which is owned by Renault).

- ⮑ Customer teams are teams that buy their power units and some other parts, and sometimes technical support, from works teams or other car manufacturers. The current customer teams in Formula 1 are Aston Martin (Mercedes customer), Haas F1 Team (Ferrari customer), Kick Sauber (Ferrari customer), McLaren (Mercedes customer), Red Bull Racing (Honda customer), RB (Honda customer), and Williams Racing (Mercedes customer).

- ⮑ Satellite teams are closely affiliated with another team and may share resources and personnel with that team, or even use the same chassis or power unit. The current satellite team in Formula 1 is RB. RB is Red Bull Racing's junior team where they try out their younger talent for possible promotion to the senior Red Bull Racing team. This satellite team came into being when Red Bull Racing bought the Minardi team in 2004 and rebranded it as Scuderia Toro Rosso, which means "stable red bull" in Italian. In 2020, the team was rebranded to AlphaTauri (Red Bull Racing's clothing brand name). In 2024, its name was changed to RB.

➲ Privateer teams (aka independent teams) are teams that are independently owned and operated (i.e., they are not owned by a major company that can funnel money and resources into them). They typically have the smallest budgets of all the teams in Formula 1. In the earlier days of F1, they might have used another team's outdated car. Now all teams have to construct their own cars but can still purchase some of the major parts from car manufacturers. McLaren and Williams Racing fall into this category. In Chapter 8, read about rules the FIA put in place to try to make things fairer so that the independent teams have a fighting chance against their more deep-pocketed rivals.

Q: What does "Scuderia" mean?

A: The team often referred to as simply Ferrari is actually called Scuderia Ferrari. Scuderia means stable in Italian, as in a horse stable.

Q: What is a technical directive?

A: F1 has an extensive rulebook that is updated every season. But rules can sometimes be interpreted in different ways. If a team asks for clarification on a rule, the FIA will issue a technical directive to clarify the rule.

Q: What is a run off area?

A: A run-off area is an area between the track and any barriers, made of a material that has more friction than the track itself to slow down any cars that run off the track (thus the name). Many are high-friction asphalt, but there are still old-school gravel and grass run-off areas on some circuits.

Q: What is the start/finish?

A: In a closed-circuit race (which all F1 races are), the start and finish lines of the race are one and the same. This line is referred to as the start/finish.

Q: What are the different types of qualifying laps in Formula 1?

A: During the laps of an actual race, drivers go as fast as they can under the circumstances on the track. But during qualifying, there are three different types of laps during which the drivers may behave differently than in a race. These are three types of qualifying lap:

- Out-lap—This is the first lap around the track during qualifying or practice after a driver leaves the garage (which is right behind the pit for each driver, on the other side of the pit lane from the racetrack). It is taken slower than a regular lap and the drivers often weave the car back and forth for a reason you can read about in Chapter 6.

- Hot lap (aka push lap or flying lap)—This is a lap around the track at full speed. After the out-lap, the driver can take one or more hot laps around the track. During qualifying, the speed of their best hot lap is compared to those of other drivers and used to decide the driver's starting position on the grid.

➲ In-lap—This is the last lap of the qualifying or practice round, when the driver brings the car back to the team's garage. Like the out-lap, this lap is also taken more slowly to cool down the brakes and tires.

ⓔ❜ What is a reconnaissance lap?

🄰❜ A reconnaissance lap is taken around the track just after leaving the pits but before the cars first line up on the grid to check that the car is in good working order and to check on current track conditions, which can inform decisions like what tires to start on. A driver can opt to do more than one reconnaissance lap, but if they do, they have to divert themselves into the pit lane to avoid the cars and F1 crew standing around their team members on the grid.

ⓔ❜ When is a formation lap taken?

🄰❜ Before a race and after all the cars have initially lined up in position on the grid, all the cars take one slow lap around the track, called a "formation lap," and line up into position on the grid again. A formation lap is also taken when the cars are getting back into their spots on the track after a stopped race resumes, for instance after a red flag incident (see Chapter 5 for more information on flags).

ⓔ❜ What is a practice start?

🄰❜ A practice start is when a driver stops in an area just beyond the pit wall and then takes off at a more normal lap speed from that position before formation. It provides a quick extra practice lap that lets the car get up to speed, warms the tires and brakes, and gives the driver and team valuable data that could prove advantageous during the actual race.

Q: What is unlapping?

A: Lapped drivers are drivers at the back of the pack who have been passed by drivers at the lead of the race by an entire lap, which puts the lapped drivers in between the lead cars and other cars that are truly ahead of them but physically behind them. When a race is stopped and restarted, or when a safety car is out for any reason, sometimes lapped drivers are ordered to unlap themselves, which means they pass the lead racers who lapped them and rejoin the back of the pack in their actual race positions so that everyone is physically on the track in their true race position. When a driver is described as having unlapped themselves, it means that they had been lapped, but they caught back up and gained their lap back.

Q: What is overtaking?

A: Overtaking is another word for passing. When one F1 car passes another, you might hear that the driver has overtaken the other.

Q: What is the racing line?

A: The racing line is the imaginary line around the racetrack that would result in the perfect lap, the one that would allow for maximum speed in corners and straightaways, producing the best resulting time.

Q: What is a filming day in F1?

A: There are tight rules and restrictions regarding when the cars that will be used in actual Formula 1 races can be driven. A filming day is a day the FIA allows teams to drive their official season cars to take promotional footage. It's also a way for them to sneak in some extra testing of the car, but there are strict limits on how far they are allowed to drive. In most recent seasons, the limit was 100 kilometers (62 miles). For 2024, the limit was increased to 200 kilometers (124 miles). They also can't do all that driving on the same day. It has to take place during two days within the season. On filming days, the cars are fitted with special Pirelli tires that are hard and long lasting, unlike the soft and often replaced slicks used during races when it's not raining (see Chapter 4 for more on tire types and rules).

CHAPTER 2

TRIP DOWN MEMORY LANE
HISTORY OF THE SPORT

𝑄: When was the first known automobile race?

𝐴: Gasoline-fueled cars were invented in the mid-1880s, and not terribly long afterward, people began racing them! The first known car race was a nearly 732-mile road race from Paris to Bordeaux in 1895, though an earlier competition, which was more of a test run for the automobiles, took place in 1894 in a roughly 50-mile stretch from Paris to Rouen. At the time, automobiles weren't terribly fast. The average speed of the winner of the 1895 race was reportedly a mere 15 miles per hour.

𝑄: What was the first organized automobile race in the United States?

𝐴: The first known organized auto race in the United States was on Thanksgiving in 1895, on an approximately 54-mile route from Chicago to Evanston in the state of Illinois.

𝑄: What was the first closed-circuit road race?

𝐴: Early races had drivers starting a race at one location and ending in another, often from one town to another. In 1898, the first closed-circuit race was driven, called the Course de Périgueux. Closed-circuit means the racing route forms a loop that the drivers can traverse repeatedly. We call each iteration around the loop a lap. In a closed-circuit race, the start and finish points are one and the same.

𝑄: What was the first dedicated motorsport racetrack?

𝐴: Since there were no dedicated racetracks just after the car was invented, the earliest races took place on roads also used by the general public. This was rather dangerous for drivers, spectators, and innocent bystanders alike, including pedestrians, horse and carriage riders, and animals that might venture into the road. So it's no wonder someone eventually thought to build a dedicated racetrack on land that wasn't open to the public.

Although auto racing arguably started in France, the country didn't build its first dedicated motorsport racing track until L'autodrome de Linas Montlhéry in 1925. There are actually two locations that are contenders for the title of first purpose-built motor racing track in the world. In 1905, James Robert Crooke built a motor racing circuit at Aspendale Park in Victoria, Australia, inside an existing horseracing track. The first race on the interior car track was in 1906, and the circuit lap distance was about a mile. Horseraces continued on the surrounding track until 1931.

In 1951 the whole area was developed into residential property. Its start as a horseracing track is likely why another track, Brooklands racing circuit in England, is most often cited as the first purpose-built motor-racing track. Brooklands was constructed from 1906 to 1907 by Hugh and Ethel Locke King on their property in Weybridge, Surrey, for the sole purpose of motor racing. The track was 3.25 miles long and was designed by military man Colonel HCL Holden for maximizing both speed and safety. And the lead car on the very first jaunt around the track was an Itala driven by Ethel Locke King herself!

Q: When and where was the first official F1 race?

A: The first official Formula 1 race was in April 1950 in Pau, France, but it didn't count toward the first World Championship. The first championship F1 race was May 13, 1950, during the

British Grand Prix at the Silverstone circuit near Silverstone, England.

🅠 Why was the first race at Silverstone dubbed the "Mutton Grand Prix?"

🅐 In 1947, three years before Formula 1 came into official being, the Silverstone circuit held its first race, although an amateur one. Maurice Geoghegan organized a race between himself and 11 friends on the roads around the old Royal Air Force airfield, which was abandoned after World War II. Unfortunately, several local sheep wandered onto the tracks during the race, and Geoghegan struck and killed one of the innocent beasts. The event was henceforth dubbed the "Mutton Grand Prix."

🅠 What is the location of the oldest F1 circuit?

🅐 The Autodromo Nazionale Monza in Milan, Italy, goes through a large park on the outskirts of the city. Most often simply referred to as "Monza," it is the oldest official Formula 1 circuit. Although it was the last to hold a Grand Prix in Formula 1's inaugural year, the track was opened in September 1922, before any of the other circuits used during or since the 1950 season. Monza is most often cited as the third purpose-built motorsport track in the world behind Brooklands, which opened in 1907, and the Indianapolis Motor Speedway, which opened in 1909 (see entries in Chapters 3 and 11 for details on the Indy500 and its history in Formula 1). The original track at Monza took a mere 110 days to construct. Like many of the old circuits, it has gone through changes over the years; for instance, it used to include some truly dangerous banked curves that have been removed.

𝒬፧ What four original 1950 F1 Grand Prix circuits still host Formula 1 races to this day?

𝒜፧ Four circuits have hosted Formula 1 races from 1950 to present (as of this writing). The tracks have changed to keep up with the times, but they are still in their original locations. They are:

⮑ Silverstone Circuit in Northamptonshire, England

⮑ Circuit de Monaco in Monte Carlo, Monaco

⮑ Circuit de Spa-Francorchamps in Stavelot, Belgium

⮑ Autodromo Nazionale di Monza in Milan, Italy

𝒬፧ What nearly cost Juan Manuel Fangio first place at the 1957 German Grand Prix?

𝒜፧ Juan Manuel Fangio, whose F1 driving career spanned the 1950s, is considered one of the best F1 drivers in history. He won five World Championship titles and came in first in 24 of 51 championship Grands Prix driving for four different teams. At the 1957 German GP at Nürburgring, he nearly lost the podium while driving for Maserati when a pit stop went wrong and cost him almost a minute (an enormous amount of time in a sport known for fast pit stops and racers sometimes finishing within milliseconds of each other). Two Ferrari drivers, Mike Hawthorn and Peter Collins, got ahead of him. But Fangio's driving skills and propensity for breaking speed records saved the day, and, in a performance often cited as one of the greatest F1 feats of all time, he overtook his rivals and came in first! He retired from the sport just after the 1957 season.

Q: What F1 driver was the first to win back-to-back championships?

A: Italian racer Alberto Ascari, driving for Ferrari, came in first in six of the eight championship races in the 1952 Formula 1 season. Then, during the 1953 season, he won five of the nine championship races. This made him the first driver to achieve F1 World Champion status for two successive seasons.

Q: What was Alberto Ascari's nickname with Italian fans?

A: In Italy, fans of Alberto Ascari referred to him as "Ciccio," which means "chubby."

Q: What superstitions did Alberto Ascari hold?

A: F1 driver Alberto Ascari may have seemed fearless on the track, but he had a few superstitious fears. He was afraid of numbers he deemed unlucky and of black cats. He also wouldn't let anyone touch the case in which he kept his racing outfit.

Q: What pair of father and son race car drivers died in eerily similar circumstances?

A: Italian Formula 1 driver Alberto Ascari was the son of Antonio Ascari, a European race champion who raced from 1919 to 1925 and won 13 championships. He survived one terrible crash but was killed four days later in another during the French Grand Prix at Montlhery. Alberto was seven years old when his father died, but eventually he went into Formula 1 racing. Like his father, he won 13 championships. But unfortunately, also like his father and despite being known as a very careful driver, he was killed in an accident just four days after surviving another accident. At the 1955 Monaco Grand Prix, he lost control of his car and sank into the Mediterranean Sea! But he was fished out by a recovery crew alive, and the worst of his injuries was a broken nose. Just four days later, he went to Monza to observe a Ferrari practice session and asked if he could drive it. On the third lap, he crashed on a corner and died. Race car driving was dangerous, especially in the early days of F1, but there were several eerie similarities between the deaths of Antonio and Alberto Ascari 30 years apart: both had 13 championship Grands Prix wins, both died from crashes on left-hand corners, both fatal accidents took place just four days after they survived other potentially fatal accidents, and both died at the age of 36!

Q: What wartime business was started by race car drivers Alberto Ascari and Luigi Villoresi?

A: During World War II, when Ascari's Fiat dealership in Milan was enlisted to work on military vehicles, Ascari and fellow racer Villoresi also went into business together transporting fuel to the Italian military stationed in North Africa.

Q: What driver finally broke Juan Manuel Fangio's championship record?

A: Juan Manual Fangio held the F1 record for most Grand Prix victories at 24, until he was finally unseated by Jim Clark in 1968 after his twenty-fifth win, which occurred during the first race of the season at the South Africa Grand Prix.

Q: Who was the first British F1 World Champion?

A: John Michael Hawthorn (known as Mike Hawthorn) won his first F1 Grand Prix victory in 1953, his first year as an F1 driver, at the French Grand Prix at Reims driving for Ferrari.

But he didn't become World Champion until the 1958 season, when he ranked ahead of Stirling Moss by a single point. It was a rough year during which he saw his close friend and fellow racer Peter Collins killed in a crash at Nürburgring during the German Grand Prix. Hawthorn retired at the end of the season.

Q: What led Mike Hawthorn to become a race car driver?

A: Mike Hawthorn's father was a motorbike racer who bought and ran an auto shop near the Brooklands circuit (see earlier in this chaper for more on Brooklands). Growing up around his father's shop and near a racetrack gave him a love of motorsports that led him to decide to become a driver at the age of nine.

Q: What were Mike Hawthorn's nicknames?

A: Mike Hawthorn was known as "the Farnham Flyer." His family's auto garage was located in Farnham, Surrey, England, near the Brooklands circuit. But in France he was referred to as "le Papillon" (meaning "the butterfly").

Q: What accessory was Mike Hawthorn known to wear while racing?

A: Starting with his first single-seater race in an F2 vehicle at the Easter Meeting at the Goodwood circuit in 1952, Mike Hawthorn donned a bow tie while racing. Formula 2 is the tier of single-seater racing just below Formula 1 in the FIA racing hierarchy (see Chapter 11 for more details).

Q: How did Mike Hawthorn die?

A: Sadly, Mike Hawthorn was killed not long after becoming the 1958 World Champion, when, driving too fast on a wet road near his home, he slid and crashed his Jaguar.

Q: Who is the only driver to become World Champion in a car of his own make?

A: John Arthur Brabham (known as "Jack Brabham") trained as an engineer, worked engineering and garage jobs, and during World War II became a flight mechanic for the Royal Australian Air Force. After the war, his uncle built him a shop and he opened his own engineering business. He helped a driver friend of his build a race car and not long after began racing the car himself. Brabham won four Australian championships in a row in midget cars (a class of very small racecars) he constructed. He then drove a Cooper Bristol car to victory at the 1951 Australian Championship hill-climb competition. This led to him meeting with Charles and John Cooper, founders of the Cooper Car Company. After this meeting, he worked with them to develop rear-engine F1 cars.

In the early 1960s he started his own company, Motor Racing Developments, with Ron Tauranac, building Formula 1 and Formula 2 vehicles. In 1966, the F1 rules changed to allow a 3-liter engine, and Brabham convinced Repco (an Australian engine manufacturer) to make a Formula 1 engine based on the engine of the Oldsmobile V8. With this new engine, he built the car known as the Brabham-Repco. He went on to win the 1966 World Championship, the first F1 racer to become champion in a car developed by (and named for) himself.

ℚ? What other mode of transportation was Brabham known to "drive"?

𝒜? Jack Brabham wasn't just a race car driver. He became a pilot, as well, and would fly himself and teammates to races. He ran his own aviation company after retiring from F1 in 1970.

ℚ? What high honor outside of racing wins did Jack Brabham receive?

𝒜? Australian driver Jack Brabham was the first F1 driver to be knighted, an honor he received in 1979, making him Sir Jack Brabham.

ℚ? What other drivers have been knighted?

𝒜? Aside from Jack Brabham, three other Formula 1 drivers have been knighted. Stirling Moss was knighted in 2000, Jackie Stewart (who also received an Order of the British Empire [OBE] in 1972) was knighted in 2001, and Lewis Hamilton was knighted in 2021.

ℚ? What driver did Queen Elizabeth II refuse to let drive her to a barbecue?

𝒜? Formula 1 driver Jackie Stewart was friends with the late monarch Queen Elizabeth II after he invited her to Silverstone, where she reportedly took a spin around the track in a race car and sat in one of the Formula 1 cars. The World Champion driver reportedly offered to drive her to a barbecue sometime after his 1973 World Championship victory, but she refused, doing the driving herself but offering to let Stewart navigate.

Q: What stunt did Jack Brabham pull at the beginning of his first race after turning 40?

A: Jack Brabham was sometimes called "Geriatric Jack" due to being one of the older drivers in the 1960s. A good sport, the 40-year-old donned a long fake beard and walked to his car with a cane at the start of the 1966 Dutch Grand Prix at Zandvoort. He ditched the props before taking off and came in first in the race.

Q: What other nickname did Jack Brabham have?

A: For his dark hair and taciturn nature, Jack Brabham was known as "Black Jack."

Q: What race had the closest finish in F1 history?

A: At the 1971 Italian Grand Prix at Monza, Peter Gethin beat out Ronnie Peterson for first place by a mere one-hundredth of a second! In fact, the first five cars all crossed the finish line within less than a second.

Q: What F1 team has been most successful in the history of the sport?

A: Ferrari has thus far been the most successful team in the history of F1, with fifteen of their drivers having won Drivers' World Championship titles and the team having won 16 Constructors' World Championships.

Q: What was the last independent team to compete in Formula 1?

A: Frank Williams drove in lower-level Formula competitions in the 1960s and provided cars to Piers Courage to race during the

1969 and 1970 Formula 1 seasons (see Chapter 12 for details of the tragic end of Courage's Formula 1 career). In 1977, Williams and engineer Patrick Head founded Williams Grand Prix Engineering and entered a March car. In 1978, they got backing from Saudi Arabian Airlines, developed a Williams vehicle, and enlisted Australian driver Alan Jones. The next year they added Swiss driver Clay Regazzoni and entered two cars, a new Williams FW07 with ground-effect (see Chapter 6 for more on this innovation). Each current Formula 1 team consists of just two drivers in a given race. But this wasn't always the case (see below).

Williams won the Constructors' World Championships in 1979, 1980, and 1981, their driver Jones won the Drivers' World Championship in 1980 and driver Keke Rosberg won the Drivers' World Championship in 1982. The Williams team competed in F1 under the leadership of Frank Williams for years to come, and in 2013, his daughter Claire Williams took over day-to-day management as Deputy Team Principal, until 2020 when it was sold to an American consortium. The team still competes in Formula 1 but is no longer an independent family-owned team.

Q: What race was conducted during the hottest day in the region on record, making it the hottest F1 GP?

A: During the 2005 Bahrain Grand Prix, the temperature reached a staggering 108.5 degrees Fahrenheit, making it the hottest day on record in the region at the time, and the hottest day of any Formula GP up to that point. But the race went on, with Renault driver Fernando Alonso coming in first, followed by Toyota driver Jarno Trulli in second and McLaren's Kimi Raikkonen in third.

CHAPTER 3

THE DRIVING FORCE
DRIVERS AND TEAMS

Q: How many drivers are on each F1 team?

A: Each Formula 1 team consists of just two drivers in a given race.

Q: Who won the first Formula 1 World Championship?

A: Giuseppe Antonio Farina (known as Nino Farina) was the first World Champion in Formula 1 history. He won the first F1 World Championship in 1950 driving for the Alfa Romeo team.

Q: What group of drivers was known as "the three F's?"

A: The 1950 Alfa Romeo team consisted of Nino Farina, Juan Manuel Fangio, and Luigi Fagioli. All of their last names began with the letter F, so they were dubbed "the three F's." And they took first, second, and third places in the first F1 World Championship.

Q: What F1 driver became a car mechanic at the age of 11?

A: Juan Manuel Fangio, born in 1911, began working on cars when he was only 11 years old!

Q: Which early F1 champion had a doctorate?

A: Before his career as a Formula 1 World Champion racer, Giuseppe Antonio "Nino" Farina attended the University of Turin and obtained a degree in law and a doctorate in political economy.

Q: What early F1 driver was known as the "Racing Dentist?"

A: Charles Anthony Standish Brooks (more commonly known as "Tony Brooks") was raised in Dukinfield, Cheshire, England, by parents who were both into sports cars. In fact, he entered his first race at Goodwood in 1952, driving his mother's Healy Silverstone vehicle. At that point, he had already been studying dentistry at Manchester University (following in his dentist father's footsteps). In his last year of dental school, he took the wheel of a Formula 1 vehicle for the very first time, a Connaught, at the nonchampionship 1955 Syracuse Grand Prix in Sicily. And against all odds, he won, making him the first British driver to win a GP in a British car after WWII. After that stunning victory, he went right back to school. He continued both racing and his dentistry studies until he received his degree at the end of 1956. Over his 1956 to 1961 Formula 1 career, he took six Grand Prix victories. Dubbed the "Racing Dentist," he did not actually end up practicing dentistry and instead made his living at racing, and later running a gas station that he expanded into a car dealership, from which he retired in 1993. Brooks passed away in 2022 at the age of 90 as the last remaining 1950s Formula 1 champion.

Q: What were the nicknames of F1 World Champion Juan Manuel Fangio?

A: When F1 was formalized as a sport in 1950, Argentinian race car driver Juan Manuel Fangio was already in his late thirties. An incredibly accomplished driver, he earned the title of World Champion in Formula 1 five times and broke many records before he won his final title in 1957. Older than most other Formula 1 drivers, he was dubbed "Old Man." But that wasn't his only nickname. He was also known as "El Chueco," which means "the crooked" or "the bow-legged," due to his physique. And younger fellow driver Stirling Moss called Fangio, who was a father figure to him, "Maestro."

Q: What crowd-pleasing racing move was Juan Manuel Fangio known for?

A: Drifting may have entered the public lexicon when *The Fast and the Furious: Tokyo Drift* came out in 2006, but it has been part of the sport of racing for decades. 1950s F1 driver Juan Manuel Fangio was known to slide his car in a controlled drift on all four wheels.

Q: What injury did Juan Manuel Fangio suffer in his only serious racing accident?

A: By racing standards, Juan Manuel Fangio was a very safe driver. But he suffered a severe injury at a nonchampionship at Monza in 1952 when he wrecked his Maserati. In fact, he broke his neck! His entire upper torso was stiff for the rest of his life as a result, but it could have been worse. The crash was possibly due to exhaustion from a long drive to reach the competition.

Q: Who is considered by many as the best Formula 1 driver who never won a World Championship?

A: Stirling Moss raced Formula 1 from 1951 to 1962. He was a fantastic driver and was one of the first (maybe *the* first) Formula 1 driver to become world famous. He earned the nickname "Mr. Motor Racing." But he never managed to win a World Champion title. A crash knocked him out of Formula 1, although he did race in other motorsports once he recovered.

Q: What noble act cost Stirling Moss the 1958 World Championship?

A: At the 1958 Portuguese Grand Prix, Stirling Moss got pole position and led most of the race, followed by Mike Hawthorn. Hawthorn spun off onto a side road and stalled, and Moss stopped to see if he needed help. Hawthorn got going again and ultimately came in second behind Moss. But Hawthorn was accused of push-starting against traffic and was facing disqualification. Moss defended Hawthorn, attesting that he had backed up on a parallel road, not on the racetrack. As a result, Hawthorn got to keep his points. Hawthorn went on to win the World Championship that year by a single point!

Q: What F1 driver was kidnapped by Fidel Castro's rebels?

A: The island nation of Cuba hosted three Grands Prix called the "Gran Premio de Cuba" in 1957, 1958, and 1960. During the 1958 Grand Prix, Cuba was in the midst of a revolution led by Fidel Castro against its then leader, Fulgencio Batista. In an effort to embarrass Batista, Castro's rebels kidnapped Juan Manuel Fangio at gunpoint while he was signing autographs at the Hotel Lincoln, where he and the other drivers were staying. Thankfully, they meant him no harm and only wanted to show the world that they were serious about the revolution, but also were not the murderous group Batista was making them out to be.

Fangio was kept in a suburban area, provided with dinner and a radio so that he could listen to the race he was missing (which was delayed, but did start without him). He even signed autographs for some of his captors. Fangio reportedly talked them out of also kidnapping Stirling Moss by lying and saying he was on his honeymoon, and it wouldn't look good. The rebels holding Fangio agreed to meet with the Argentinian ambassador, to whom Fangio was released unharmed. One of the captors even reportedly gave the ambassador a letter apologizing for the incident. Fangio never gave up the identities of his captors or the location of his captivity.

Unbelievably, that wasn't the only drama that plagued the 1958 Cuban Grand Prix. Driver Hans Tanner, along with a few crew members, were arrested for having beards (which was apparently a sign that you were one of the revolutionaries) and had to be bailed out. And worst of all, the GP itself ended in a horrific disaster (see Chapter 12 for more on the tragic event that resulted in cancellation of the race amid multiple fatalities).

Q& What driver and aristocrat raced under a pseudonym and had a decidedly nonaristocratic nickname?

A& Count Wolfgang Alexander Albert Eduard Maximillian Reichsgraf Berghe von Trips was a German nobleman whose family occupied the castle Burg Hemmersbach in the Rhineland, near the Nürburgring racing circuit. After WWII, he raced motorcycles then moved on to sports cars, including at the 1954 Mille Miglia and the disaster-stricken 1955 24 Hours of Le Mans endurance race. Von Trips was offered a spot on the Ferrari Formula 1 team in 1956. He was knocked out of racing for a year due to a broken arm at Monza. He truly started racing for Ferrari in 1957, and drove his first full season in 1960. Unfortunately, he was killed in an accident at Monza the following year (see Chapter 12 for more on this terrible tragedy). In his early racing days, not wanting to draw attention to his title, von Trip entered races under the pseudonym Alex Linther. And fellow drivers called him "Taffy." It is uncertain where the nickname originated, but some say he was given this Welsh nickname by British driver and Ferrari teammate Mike Hawthorn because he thought von Trips looked Welsh.

🅠 Who was the first World Champion from the United States?

🅐 The first American driver to win an F1 World Championship was Phil Hill, who was born in 1927 in Miami, Florida. He moved to Los Angeles, California, to work in an auto garage owned by an amateur race car driver and got into two-seater racing after modifying his own MG-TC car. With an inheritance a few years later, he bought a Ferrari, with which he raced and often won. He went on to race Ferraris for other owners. In 1955, he participated in that year's infamous 24-hour race at Le Mans (see Chapter 12 for the terrible details). In 1958, he was invited to drive Formula 1 for the first time on team Ferrari. He won the Italian Grand Prix at Monza in 1960 and the 1961 Italian Grand Prix, as well, but under sad circumstances (see Chapter 12 for the fate of Hill's teammate, Count Wolfgang von Trips). Hill won the World Championship for the 1961 season, making him the first American World Champion.

🅠 Which driver lapped all but one other driver in the 1963 Belgian Grand Prix?

🅐 In the 1963 Belgian Grand Prix, despite wet road conditions and having started in eighth position, Jim Clark zoomed into the lead and never left. He even managed to get a lap ahead of all but one driver: Bruce McLaren, who came in second. Clark came in first with an astonishing four-minute and 54-second lead time on McLaren.

Q: What post-retirement career did F1 driver Phil Hill have?

A: While he was an F1 driver, he was a hobbyist at restoring both old vehicles as well as vintage player pianos (the kinds that play themselves). After retiring from F1 in 1964 and all racing in 1967, he kept restoring old cars, but this time as a successful career.

Q: How did Nino Farina die?

A: First World Champion F1 driver Nino Farina was known for driving recklessly and having a lot of accidents on the track. And he did, indeed, die in a car accident—but not during a race! In 1966, 11 years after he retired from racing to become an Alfa Romeo dealer, his Lotus-Cortina slipped off a slick road in the Alps near Chambery, on his way to the French Grand Prix. He did not survive the accident.

Q: What insignia did British racer Graham Hill wear on his helmet?

A: Londoner Norman Graham Hill (aka Graham Hill) was a member of the London Rowing Club shortly before embarking on his F1 career. The club had an insignia of eight vertical stripes meant to signify the eight oars used by the eight rowers on a racing boat. Hill added this insignia to his race helmet.

Q: Who was the only driver to have won the Triple Crown of motorsports?

A: In motorsports, the Triple Crown refers to winning F1 at Monaco (or sometimes the Formula 1 Driver's Grand Champion title), the 24 Hours of Le Mans endurance race, and the Indianapolis 500 (all considered the pinnacle of their field of motorsport). After winning Le Mans in 1972, British driver Norman Graham Hill became the first racer to come in first in all three. As of this writing, no one else has achieved this feat, although several have managed two of the three wins.

Q: How was Norman Graham Hill killed?

A: Norman Graham Hill died in a crash in 1975, but it wasn't a car crash. He was flying his own small Piper Aztec plane, purchased in 1966 with his winnings from his Indy500 victory, into Elstree airfield outside of London in a thick fog when it hit trees at a nearby golf course and crashed. He and his five passengers, all fellow members of the Embassy Hill Formula 1 team, were killed, including young up-and-coming driver Tony Brise. Embassy Hill only had nine team members, including crew, so this sad event effectively wiped out the team.

Q: Who was the first World Champion in both F1 and motorcycle racing?

A: British driver John Surtees, born in 1934, got his start in motorcycle racing at the age of 17. From 1956 to 1960, he achieved seven World Championship wins in the sport. Near the end of his motorcycle racing career, he began testing single-seater race vehicles, then racing Formula 3 (see Chapter 11 for more details on this F1 feeder motorsport). He began his Formula 1 career a little over halfway through the 1960 season as a driver for Lotus. He won the Driver's World Championship title for the 1964 season, making him the first World Championship driver in both motorbike and car racing. In fact, as of this writing, he's still the only driver to make this achievement.

Q: What driver was known to have a naughty patch on his driving uniform?

A: British driver James Hunt, who drove Formula 1 from 1973 to 1979, famously wore a patch on the front of his driving suit that read "Sex, Breakfast of Champions."

Q: What French driver's parents changed his name to prevent him from being sent to a concentration camp?

A: French driver François Cevert's father was a member of the French Resistance during World War II, and also Jewish. Cevert was born with the last name "Goldenberg." His parents changed their children's names, fearing that it would get them sent to a Nazi concentration camp. He survived the war, but see Chapter 12 for more on his tragic end after a promising start as a Formula 1 driver.

Q: What new team is being considered by the FIA and Formula 1 to become an 11th team in the sport?

A: In 2023, the FIA started accepting applications for all new Formula 1 teams. One of the contenders is Andretti Cadillac, a partnership between Andretti Autosport (run by former F1 driver Michael Andretti, son of another famous F1 driver, Mario Andretti) and Cadillac, a subsidiary of General Motors. Andretti Cadillac had hoped to start Formula 1 for the 2025 season, and their bid was accepted by the FIA but rejected by Formula 1, in part because the organization thought the team might not be able to handle designing new F1 cars for both the 2025 season and the 2026 season, the latter of which will see a lot of rule and specification changes. The prospective Andretti Cadillac team is now focusing on entering Formula 1 for the 2026 season. Andretti Autosport teams already compete in Formula E, IndyCar, and other race series (see Chapter 11 for more on these other single-seater racing series).

Q: What driver drove in an F1 race he wasn't supposed to be in?

A: Hans Heyer from Germany was an accomplished driver in touring and sports car driving, but his short career in F1 was noteworthy only for a stunt he pulled in his first (and only) race at the German Grand Prix in Hockenheim in 1977. Driving for new team ATS, he failed to qualify but was slated as first reserve driver (in case one of the two main drivers had to quit for any reason, like injury or illness). When the actual race started, he jumped in with his own car and managed to do nine laps before a gearbox issue forced him to stop. Because he didn't finish the race, he was given a black flag. But even if that hadn't happened, he would have been disqualified because he wasn't supposed to be there in the first place.

Q: In what F1 races did the driver in last place take first and win the race?

A: There have been six times in F1 history when a driver in last place raced to the front of the pack and took first place:

- David Coulthard driving for McLaren in the 2003 Australian Grand Prix

- Giancarlo Fisichella driving for Jordan in the 2003 Brazilian Grand Prix

- Fernando Alonso driving for Renault in the 2008 Singapore Grand Prix

➲ Jenson Button driving for McLaren in the 2010 Australian Grand Prix

➲ Jenson Button for McLaren (again!) in the 2011 Canadian Grand Prix

➲ Sergio Perez driving for Racing Point in the 2020 Sakhir Grand Prix

℮ Who holds the record for winning a race from the farthest starting position back?

Ⓐ 1983, John Watson, driving for McLaren in the United States Grand Prix West in Long Beach, California, started the race in the 22nd position on the grid but managed to zoom to first place, winning first while his teammate Niki Lauda took second and Rene Arnoux of Ferrari took third. This makes Watson the person who has won a race from the farthest starting position from pole. And his record will be tough to beat, at least in modern times, because as of this writing there are only 10 teams, and with two drivers per team, there are only 20 starting positions in any modern F1 race. Perhaps if and when Team Andretti begins competing, someone can attempt the same feat (see the team Andretti Cadillac entry earlier in this chapter).

℮ Who is the only driver to qualify for pole position three times but never lead any laps?

Ⓐ Italian driver Teo Fabi was talented enough to qualify for pole position three times in his career, which ran from 1985 to 1987. He started in pole position at the 1985 German Grand Prix in Nürburgring, and in the Austrian and Italian Grands Prix in 1986. But astonishingly, he never crossed the finish line first in any lap during any race. He came close once when he was leading lap 17 at the 1986 Austrian Grand Prix, only for his engine to fail before the end of the lap. Despite this unfortunate record, Fabi wasn't a backmarker driver. He came in second in 56 laps and managed to take two third place podiums, one at the 1984 Detroit Grand Prix and the other at the 1987 Austrian Grand Prix.

Q: What three drivers once tied for pole position in the European Grand Prix?

A: In the 1997 European Grand Prix at Circuito Permanente de Jerez in Spain, drivers Heinz-Harald Frentzen, Michael Schumacher, and Jacques Villeneuve all had lap times of 1 minute and 21.072 seconds in the qualifying session, which had never happened before (or since, for that matter). Normally the driver with the best lap time gets pole position; when drivers tie, they go with the order in which the drivers set the lap time. In this case, it was Villeneuve, then Schumacher, then Frentzen. So Villeneuve got pole position.

Q: Which driver passed the lead driver in the last lap of the 2005 Japanese Grand Prix?

A: In 2005 at the Japanese Grand Prix in Suzuka, Renault driver Giancarlo Fisichella was in the lead over half the race and was expected to win. But McLaren driver Kimi Raikkonen, who started seventeenth on the grid, overtook Fisichella on the very last lap and took first place in a surprise upset.

Q: Who holds the record for most Grand Slams?

A: Scottish F1 driver Jim Clark achieved eight Grand Slams before his untimely death in 1968 during a Formula 2 race in

Germany. At the time of this writing, Clark still holds the Grand Slam world record.

Q: Who led over 71 percent of the laps in the 1963 F1 season?

A: Jim Clark led an astounding 71.47 percent of the laps during the 1963 Formula 1 season in his Lotus 25 car, still a record to this day.

Q: Which driver scored just one point less than the 2007 World Champion during his first year in the sport?

A: Lewis Hamilton started his Formula 1 career during the 2007 season driving for McLaren, which had begun funding him years earlier during his karting career. In his debut Formula 1 season, he was in the lead for a while, but during the final race, Ferrari driver Kimi Raikkonen beat him by a single point, taking the World Champion title. Victory wasn't far away for Hamilton, though. Read on to find out more about this skilled driver.

Q: Who overtook a driver in the last few seconds of the last 2008 Grand Prix, securing himself the Drivers' World Champion title?

A: At the 2008 Brazilian Grand Prix at Interlagos, the last Grand Prix of the season, Lewis Hamilton flew past Timo Glock, who was having trouble controlling his car due to wet track conditions, in the last few seconds of the last lap. Although Hamilton came in fifth in the race, the points gained propelled him over his closest rival Felipe Massa's points and made Hamilton the 2008 Drivers' World Champion, his first of seven titles.

Q: Which driver holds the record for winning the most World Championships?

A: As of this writing, near the end of the 2023 F1 season, two drivers are tied for this record, both having won seven World Championships each: Michael Schumacher and Lewis Hamilton. Michael Schumacher's wins took place in 1994, 1995, 2000, 2001, 2002, 2003, and 2004. And Lewis Hamilton's wins occurred in 2008, 2014, 2015, 2017, 2018, 2019, and 2020. Coincidentally, in 2013, before tying the World Championship record, Schumacher retired from Mercedes and Hamilton moved from McLaren to Mercedes to replace him.

Q: What honor outside of F1 did Lewis Hamilton receive in 2016 and 2020?

A: Lewis Hamilton was named one of *Time* magazine's Top 100 most influential people in 2016 in the Icons category, and again in 2020 in the Titans category for both his abilities on the track and his activism.

Q: Who asked Lewis Hamilton to leave McLaren for Mercedes?

A: Lewis Hamilton was funded by McLaren years before he made it to Formula 1, and once he did, he stayed with the team from 2007 through 2012. In 2012, famous retired Austrian F1 driver Niki Lauda joined the Mercedes-AMG Petronas Motorsport team as chairman (see more in this chapter and Chapter 4 on Lauda's F1 career). He made the call to Lewis Hamilton asking him to join Mercedes, which Hamilton did, starting in the 2013 season. Hamilton later stated that due to some comments Lauda made when he was a commentator, he didn't think Lauda liked

him very much. But they met and became fast friends. Lauda passed away in April 2019, just a few days before the Monaco Grand Prix. Hamilton wore a helmet in tribute to Lauda during the race.

Q: What driver has won the most individual F1 races?

A: As of this writing, Lewis Hamilton holds that record with a whopping 103 race wins. The runners up are Michael Schumacher with 91, Max Verstappen with 54, Sebastian Vettel with 53, and Alain Prost with 51.

Q: Which driver has had the most podium finishes in F1?

A: As of the end of the 2023 season, Lewis Hamilton also holds this record with 197 podium finishes under his belt.

Q: Which driver has thus far held the most pole positions?

A: Once again, as of the 2023 season, Lewis Hamilton has the record for holding the most pole positions at 104.

Q: Who is the first Black F1 driver?

A: The first Black F1 driver is Lewis Hamilton, born in Stevenage, England, in 1985. His father's parents hailed from the country of Grenada. Like many racers, he got his start in karting as a kid, and he has raced in Formula 1 since 2007. Hamilton is a staunch supporter of equality and diversity. He has led support for the Black Lives Matter movement by taking the knee before each F1 race (and some, but not all, other drivers have followed his lead). Hamilton also commissioned a study into diversity in Formula 1 that found that only 1 percent of people working in the sport are Black.

Q: Who was the first female F1 Grand Prix driver?

A: Italian driver Maria Teresa de Filippis was the first woman to race in Formula 1. Born in Naples, she got into sports car racing after her brothers bet that she couldn't drive fast enough, and they were proven wrong when she won. From 1958 to 1959, she competed in five Formula 1 Grands Prix for the Maserati team, qualifying for and starting three of them. She left Formula 1 when her team boss, Jean Behra, passed away. In 1979, she joined a club for retired F1 drivers, the Club Internationale des Anciens Pilotes de Grand Prix F1, and was named honorary president.

Q: Who was the first female F1 racer to score points?

A: Italian driver Maria Grazia Lombardi (aka Lella Lombardi), born in 1941 in Frugarolo, was the first and, in fact, only woman thus far, to score points in Formula 1. Like many Formula 1 drivers, she started in karting and then stepped into various other series. She became World Champion in Formula 850 after winning four races and went on to race F3, Celebrity Escort Mexicos, and the US F5000 series, and eventually stepped up to F1 driving for the March Engineering team. Lombardi participated in 17 Grands Prix and qualified for and started 12 of the races from 1974 to 1976. She came in sixth in the 1975 Spanish Grand Prix, scoring the points that gave her this distinction. Sadly, she died of breast cancer at the age of 51.

Q: How many women have driven in F1 Grand Prix events?

A: So far there have only been five women to compete in Formula 1 Grand Prix events and another more recent driver

who did not officially compete but who did practice rounds during Grand Prix weekends:

- Maria Teresa de Filippis from Italy (1958 to 1959)—5 GPs, 3 starts
- Lella Lombardi from Italy (1974 to 1976)—17 GPs, 12 starts
- Divinia Galica from Britain (1976)—qualifying round
- Desiré Wilson from South Africa (1980)—qualifying round
- Giovanna Amati from Italy (1992)—qualifying round
- Susie Wolff from Scotland (2014 to 2015)—practice rounds

Q: Who were the only known LGBTQ+ Formula 1 drivers?

A: Thus far, there have only been two known LGBTQ+ drivers, both of whom competed in the 1970s: the aforementioned Italian driver Lella Lombardi (see above entries), who was a lesbian, and driver Mike Beuttler, who was a gay man. Beuttler, who was born in Cairo, Egypt, in 1940, raced in Formula 1 from 1971 to 1973, competing in 28 races and coming in in the top 10 spots five times. The oil crisis of 1973 made it too expensive for him to compete, and he retired and moved from London to California. Sadly, he was there during the height of the AIDS epidemic that took so many lives in the community, and he died of a related illness in 1988 when he was just 48 years old.

Q: What group started in 2019 hopes to promote LGBTQ+ inclusion in motorsports?

A: When British driver Richard Morris was in karting at 14 years of age, he experienced antigay harassment when someone wrote homophobic slurs on the stickers on his kart. But he stayed in motorsports and is now the 2023 European Sports Prototype Cup Champion. Morris, who is openly gay, founded the group Racing Pride in 2019 to help promote LGBTQ+ diversity in motorsports. Aston Martin Chief Communication Officer Matt Bishop, who is also openly gay, is one of the group's founding ambassadors. Other ambassadors include drivers Abbie Eaton and Charlie Martin, among many others.

Q: What driver requested that a race be canceled due to weather, only to suffer a terrible injury when it wasn't?

A: During the 1976 German Grand Prix at Nürburgring, rain was in the forecast, and Ferrari driver Niki Lauda wanted them to cancel the race, but he was overruled. After the rain started, he crashed his car and it burst into flames, then he was struck by both Harald Ertl and Brett Lunger. They stopped and jumped out to help, as did other drivers. It took a while to get him out of the car and to the hospital. Not only did he suffer horrific burns, but he was in a coma for three weeks. But that did not deter him. Just a few weeks after the crash, he was back in the driver's seat and racing. He came in fourth place at Monza a mere 42 days after his seemingly debilitating crash!

Q: What quirky tradition does Daniel Ricciardo often do on the podium?

A: Australian driver Daniel Ricciardo has a quirky tradition called the "shoey." On the podium after a win, he drinks champagne (or sparkling wine) from his own shoe! He didn't come up with the move out of the blue, and he wasn't the first Motorsport driver to do it. The shoey originated with an Australian group called the "Mad Hueys" (surfers and fishermen who own a surfing and fishing gear company), who are known to drink beer from their shoes and swim flippers. The group hung out with Australian MotoGP rider Jack Miller, and he reportedly told them he would do a shoey the next time he won a podium spot, and he followed through after his first victory at the MotoGP Dutch TT at Assen in 2016, drinking champagne out of his boot. Miller stated that it was a bit of a dig at Honda, which had apparently reprimanded and fined the racer after he did a shoey at a party. Daniel Ricciardo, a fellow Australian, started doing the shoey the same year and the rest is history.

Q: Which lead driver was foiled in the final laps by a puncture in 1992 at Monaco?

A: In 1992 at the Monaco Grand Prix, driver Nigel Mansell spent most of the race in the lead. Unfortunately, one of his tires was slowly losing air to a puncture, forcing him to pit for new tires. He resumed the race behind Ayrton Senna and never managed to get past his rival. Mansell crossed the finish line a mere two-tenths of a second behind Senna.

ℚ℘ What fathers and sons have competed in F1?

ℚ℘ Thus far, there have been 15 sons who've followed their fathers into Formula 1 racing. Here are all the father-and-son drivers over the history of F1:

- Reg Parnell and Tim Parnell
- André Pilette and Theodore "Teddy" Pilette
- Sir Jack Brabham and David Brabham
- Mario Andretti and Michael Andretti
- Emmerson Fittipaldi and Christian Fittipaldi
- Graham Hill and Damon Hill
- Keke Rosberg and Nico Rosberg
- Gilles Villeneuve and Jacques Villeneuve
- Manfred Winkelhock and Markus Winkelhock
- Satoru Nakajima and Kazuki Nakajima
- Nelson Piquet and Nelson Piquet, Jr.
- Jan Magnussen and Kevin Magnussen
- Jos Verstappen and Max Verstappen
- Jonathan Palmer and Jolyon Palmer
- Michael Schumacher and Mick Schumacher

ℚ℘ What father-and-son F1 racers are the only ones to have both won World Champion?

ℚ℘ There have been 15 father-and-son duos to become Formula 1 drivers (see entry above). But both father and son managed to become World Champions in only one of these duos: Graham Hill (in 1962 and 1968) and his son Damon Hill (in 1996).

Q: Which father and son finished in the same slot in both their final races?

A: Graham Hill, who drove in F1 from 1958 to 1975, had a son named Damon Hill. Graham died when Damon was a child, but Damon later followed in his father's footsteps and became a Formula 1 driver. Damon even wore the same unique insignia on his helmet as his father (see earlier entries on Graham Hill for more details). In Graham Hill's final race, he finished the race in 11th place. In Damon Hill's final race (around 20 years after his father's last race), he also finished in 11th place!

Q: Who are the only brothers to have both won F1 Grands Prix?

A: Michael Schumacher is world-renowned for having won the Formula 1 World Championship seven times, a record tied by Lewis Hamilton, but not yet surpassed. But he wasn't the only Schumacher racing at the time. His younger brother, Ralf Schumacher, was a Formula 1 driver from 1997 to 2007, and in that time won six Grands Prix victories, and even stood on the podium with his brother for the 2001 Canadian Grand Prix, where Ralf took first and Michael took second!

Q: Which driver is referred to as the "Flying Finn?"

A: Finnish driver Mika Hakkinen, who won the 1998 and 1999 Formula 1 World Championships, is sometimes referred to as the "Flying Finn."

Q: Who was the youngest Formula 1 driver?

A: Max Verstappen, son of F1 driver Jos Verstappen and kart and race car driver Sophie Kumpen, began go-karting at the age of four and won his first race at seven. By 16, he was both European and World Champion. Verstappen graduated from karting to Formula 1 racing at the 2015 Australian Grand Prix when he was just 17 years old, making him the youngest F1 driver to date. He is also the youngest Grand Prix winner, having won the 2016 Spanish Grand Prix at the age of 18. Although the youngest, he is one of many Formula 1 drivers who got their start as children in karting.

Q: How old does a driver need to be in order to drive in F1 races?

A: Since a rule change not long after Max Verstappen started racing F1 at the age of 17, drivers now have to be at least 18 years of age at the time of their first Formula 1 race. This age minimum is a requirement for getting something called an F1 Super Licence, which is required to compete in F1. Read on to find out more about the Super Licence.

Q: What is a Formula 1 Super Licence and how does a driver get one?

A: A driver who has met a set of rigorous requirements and gained enough points from racing in certain other motorsports can attain an F1 Super Licence, which is issued by the FIA and required to be an F1 driver. As noted in the previous entry, in order to obtain this special license, a driver must be 18 years of age at the time of their first F1 race. Drivers must also have a regular driver's license and an International Grade A

Competition license. They must pass a written exam to ensure that they know the rules and regulations. Drivers need to have participated in at least 80 percent of two seasons of another single-seater championship (like F2, F3, or FE). They must also have attained 40 points over the last three seasons (with some extra time allowed and fewer points required if any of those seasons included the 2020 season that was truncated due to COVID-19). A set number of points is doled out for coming in first, second, or third in a number of specific racing types that feed into F1 (with each of those racing genres assigned different numbers of points). A few extra points are doled out if a driver doesn't receive any penalty points. Each driver also has to pay a hefty sum for an F1 Super Licence. Although it is hard to find reference to the exact cost, it has been reported to involve a flat fee of $12,800 plus an additional 10 percent of that base amount for each World Championship point scored.

Q: Who holds the record for youngest Formula 1 World Champion?

A: As of 2023, Sebastian Vettel holds the record for youngest World Championship winner for his 2021 victory for team Red Bull when he was 23 years and 134 days old. The runners up are Lewis Hamilton in 2008 for McLaren when he was 23 years and 300 days old, Fernando Alonso in 2005 for Renault when he was 24 years and 58 days old, Max Verstappen in 2021 for Red Bull Racing when he was 24 years and 73 days old, and Emerson Fittipaldi 1972 for Lotus when he was 25 years and 273 days old.

Q: Who won 19 of 22 Grands Prix in the 2023 F1 season?

A: Dutch driver Max Verstappen of the Red Bull Racing team won 19 out of 22 Grands Prix during the 2023 F1 season, earning him his third Drivers' World Championship title.

Q: Who was the oldest F1 Grand Prix winner?

A: Luigi Fagioli won the 1951 French Grand Prix when he was 53 years old, making him the oldest Formula 1 Grand Prix winner to date.

Q: What drivers have won the last race of the person who won their first race?

A: Thus far, there have been three sets of racers to whom this has happened:

- Alan Jones won Alain Prost's first race, and later Prost won Jones's last race.
- Alain Prost won the first race of Ayrton Senna, and Senna won Prost's last race.
- Michael Schumacher won Jenson Button's first race, and Button won Schumacher's last race.

Q: Who was the only driver from the US during the 2023 F1 season?

A: Williams team member Logan Sargeant was the only driver from the US during the 2023 Formula 1 season. Since the US now has three circuits, he was also the only racer to compete in three home races.

Q: Who was the last American driver to score points in F1?

A: Until 2023, the answer was Michael Andretti, who scored seven points during the 1993 Formula 1 season. But Logan Sargeant, who started during the 2023 season, managed to score a single point at the United States Grand Prix in Austin, Texas. He came in twelfth during the actual race, but Ferrari driver Charles Leclerc and Mercedes driver Lewis Hamilton were both disqualified when during post-race checks it was found that the planks underneath their vehicles were too worn down (see Chapter 4 for more on the plank on an F1 vehicle), which moved Sargeant to tenth place, giving him a single point.

Q: Which driver had the shortest career?

A: Mario Dominguez was one of three Jordan Grand Prix (the name of a team, not an actual Grand Prix) drivers (along with Narain Karthikeyan and Tiago Montiero) testing a car during the 2005 season at Silverstone. Karthikeyan and Montiero did most of the testing because when it was Dominguez's turn, it was too foggy and rainy for the medical helicopter to take off if a crash occurred, so all he was allowed was a slow single installation lap, and that was the extent of his F1 career. But he didn't leave racing but went back to his previous gig as a Champ Car driver and later competed in FIA's GT series. The next runner-up may be Ernest Loof, who managed to drive just two meters at the 1953 German Grand Prix before his engine died.

Q: What driver won an F1 race by the widest time margin?

A: The driver who won a race by the widest time margin in F1 history was Stirling Moss when he beat the second-place driver by over five minutes in the 1958 Portuguese Grand Prix.

Q: What drivers won F1 races by the highest lap count?

A: Two drivers hold this record—both beating their competitors by two full laps! Jackie Stewart won the Spanish Grand Prix by two full laps in 1969, and Damon Hill did the same at the Australian Grand Prix in 1995.

Q: Who was the first British driver to win a Formula 1 Grand Prix in a British-made car?

A: After British driver Tony Brooks drove a Connaught Formula 2 car with good results, Connaught enlisted him to drive their Formula 1 car at the nonchampionship 1955 Syracuse Grand Prix in Sicily. He placed first, making him the first British motorsport driver to win a race in a British car since 1924, and, of course, the first to do so as a Formula 1 driver.

Q: Who is the only motorsport driver to have won the Sports Illustrated "Sportsman of the Year" award?

A: In 1973, Jackie Stewart became the only motorsport driver to be awarded Sports Illustrated "Sportsman of the Year" (an honor now called the "Sportsperson of the Year"). And as of this writing, he's still the only one to this day.

Q: What other honors did Jackie Stewart receive in 1973?

A: Jackie Stewart was also honored with the BBC's "Sports Personality of the Year" and the Wide World of Sports "Athlete of the Year." Read on to find out what notable (and infamous) athlete with whom he shared the latter honor.

Q: Who was voted Wide World of Sports "Athlete of the Year" alongside Jackie Stewart?

A: There were two athletes selected as "Athlete of the Year" by ABC's Wide World of Sports program: F1 driver Jackie Stewart and infamous American football player OJ Simpson!

Q: What driver helped turn around Ferrari's 1973 losing streak?

A: Ferrari, despite being a founding F1 team and a renowned sports car manufacturer, did not manage to win a single Grand Prix during the 1973 season. The renowned team came in sixth in the Constructors' Championship. Their pick for driver for the 1974 season, Clay Regazoni, convinced Enzo Ferrari to sign Niki Lauda as the second driver. Lauda joined the team, made suggestions to fix an understeering problem with the car, and went on to help Ferrari become a winning team once again, with Ferrari taking the fiftieth Grand Prix win in its history. The team went on to win three Constructors' World Championship titles within four years, and during that span, Lauda won 26 races and two Drivers' World Championships.

Q: Do the winners get to keep their trophies?

A: Most winning drivers do not get the trophies handed to them after their victories. The teams usually keep them and put them on display in their headquarters, and the driver may get a replica. But it all depends on the team contracts. Some drivers do get to keep the originals.

Q: What are the rules related to each driver's race number?

A: Since 2014, each driver picks a number and, for the most part, that is their race number for the rest of their F1 career. But the World Champion at the end of the Formula 1 season can adopt the number 1 for the next F1 season. Max Verstappen, for instance, has had race number 1 since 2022 because he won the title in 2021. Prior to 2014, numbers belonged to teams rather than drivers.

Q: What 10 Formula 1 teams competed in 2023?

A: The 10 teams that competed in the 2023 F1 season are (in alphabetical order):

- Alfa Romeo
- AlphaTauri (formerly Toro Rosso)
- Alpine
- Aston Martin
- Ferrari
- Haas
- McLaren
- Mercedes
- Red Bull Racing
- Williams

Q: Who were the drivers for each 2023 F1 team?

A: The following were the drivers who competed for each 2023 F1 team:

- Alfa Romeo: Valtteri Bottas and Guanyu Zhou
- AlphaTauri: Yuki Tsunoda and Daniel Ricciardo
- Alpine: Esteban Ocon and Pierre Gasly
- Aston Martin: Fernando Alonso and Lance Stroll
- Ferrari: Charles Leclerc and Carlos Sainz
- Haas: Kevin Magnussen and Nico Hulkenberg
- McLaren: Lando Norris and Oscar Piastri
- Mercedes: Lewis Hamilton and George Russell

- Red Bull: Max Verstappen and Sergio Perez
- Williams: Alex Albon and Logan Sargeant

Q: What teams and drivers are slated to compete in the 2024 season?

A: The driver roster is unusually stable at the moment, with the drivers beginning the 2024 season being the same as those who competed to the end of the 2023 season. None of them have even switched teams, but a couple of the team names changed. The following are the teams and drivers slated to compete in 2024:

- Kick Sauber (formerly Alfa Romeo): Valtteri Bottas and Guanyu Zhou
- RB (formerly AlphaTauri): Yuki Tsunoda and Daniel Ricciardo
- Alpine: Esteban Ocon and Pierre Gasly
- Aston Martin: Fernando Alonso and Lance Stroll
- Ferrari: Charles Leclerc and Carlos Sainz
- Haas: Kevin Magnussen and Nico Hulkenberg
- McLaren: Lando Norris and Oscar Piastri
- Mercedes: Lewis Hamilton and George Russell
- Red Bull Racing: Max Verstappen and Sergio Perez
- Williams: Alex Albon and Logan Sargeant

Q: What is a silly season in Formula 1?

A: In journalism, a silly season is a period of time when there's not a lot going on news-wise so the journalists do articles about more frivolous things than usual to fill up the news cycle. This term is often used in other fields to mean similar things that go on during a period of downtime. In Formula 1, that period is during the summer break that FIA requires for F1, usually between the last race in July and a race sometime around late August. And it's not just the drivers who get a rest. During the break, for 14 consecutive days of each team's choosing, the team factory has to (mostly) shut down and not do any design, testing, planning, or parts manufacturing related to Formula 1, although necessary maintenance is allowed. The team can also keep anything unrelated to the performance of the cars going, like legal, marketing, and accounting. During this downtime, rumors fly about who's going to be signed to what team for the upcoming season.

Q: What F1 team has won the most Constructors' World Championships?

A: Ferrari, which has been a part of F1 since day one of the sport, has won a whopping 16 Constructors' World Championships. The next runners up are Williams with nine, Mercedes and McLaren with eight each, and Lotus with seven.

Q: What team holds the record for most Grand Prix wins?

A: Once again, the answer is Ferrari, which has won 242 Grands Prix as of 2023. The next runners up are McLaren with 183, Mercedes with 125, Williams with 114, and Red Bull Racing with 113.

Q: What team holds the record for most pole positions?

A: Unsurprisingly, Ferrari holds the record for most pole positions at 243 as of the 2023 season. The next record holders are

McLaren at 156, Mercedes at 137, Williams at 128, and Lotus at 107.

Q: What team did Daniel Ricciardo leave Red Bull Racing for at the end of the 2018 season?

A: Daniel Ricciardo left Red Bull for Renault after the 2018 Formula 1 season to race with them in 2019.

Q: Who is the most notable current pay driver in F1?

A: The sport used to be dominated by rich hobbyists and car companies, but since Formula 1 became more of a business and far more expensive to run, teams have had to look for ways to drum up funding to keep them going. Sometimes this funding comes in the form of pay drivers, drivers who are at least in part chosen for the money they bring with them. But that doesn't mean they can't drive. You don't last in Formula 1 if you aren't good enough to place. A notable current F1 driver who could be considered a pay driver is Lance Stroll, whose father Lawrence Stroll funded Williams during his career there, then bought Force India and rebranded it Racing Point, which subsequently ousted Esteban Ocon and brought on Lance Stroll to join driver Sergio Perez on the team for the 2020 season.

Q: Why is Formula 1 sometimes called the "piranha club?"

A: Sports are competitive by nature, and that competition doesn't always stay on the track between rival teams. Lots of drama plays out between fellow team members and in the political landscape between teams, the Formula 1 organization, and the FIA. This has led some to call it the "piranha club."

Q: What two drivers racked up massive penalties at the 2015 Belgian Grand Prix?

A: When rules are broken, the stewards dole out penalties to drivers and teams. In the 2015 Belgian Grand Prix, drivers Jenson Button and Fernando Alonso racked up 105 grid penalties because their engines were swapped out multiple times.

Q: Which F1 driver has had the most race starts without winning a race?

A: The driver in second place for this record is still racing currently: Nico Hulkenberg, who has been driving Formula 1 since 2010. Hulkenberg, a talented driver who often comes in in the top 10, has started around 200 races without ever grabbing that top podium spot. But another driver has him beat for the record. Andrea de Cesaris started 208 races in his 1980 to 1994 career but never quite managed to reach first place. Sadly, Cesaris died in a motorcycle crash in 2014. See Chapter 12 for a heartbreaking coincidence regarding the date of Cesaris's death.

Q: What driver had near fatal injuries in a 2011 accident, but made a comeback in 2023?

A: Polish driver Robert Kubica was all set to join Scuderia Ferrari for the 2012 Formula 1 season when he crashed into a guardrail at the Ronde di Andora rally in 2011. He suffered near fatal injuries, but thankfully pulled through. He returned as a reserve driver for Williams in 2018. In 2022, with the W Racing Team, he became the Le Mans Series champion, and in 2023 the FIA World Endurance Champion. And Kubica is reportedly slated to drive for Ferrari in the 2024 World Endurance Championship.

Q: What team that lasted through the 1980s had more drivers than points?

A: The Italian team Osella lasted from 1980 to 1990. During this time, they went through nearly 20 drivers. But the team as a whole only ever earned a total of five points.

Q: What Formula 1 team is owned by an energy drink company?

A: The answer is, of course, Red Bull Racing. While many teams are owned by car manufacturers, Red Bull Racing is owned by the Red Bull energy drink company. The team was previously a manufacturer team; it was Jaguar, owned by Ford, when Red Bull purchased it in 2004 and began racing as Red Bull for the 2005 season. Red Bull bought the Minardi team in 2005, which was renamed Toro Rosso (see below for more on this second team).

Q: What driver retired from Formula 1 in 2018 but later came back?

A: During the summer break of the 2018 season, Fernando Alonso announced that he was retiring from Formula 1 racing at the end of the season. He didn't, however, retire from racing entirely. Even before he left Formula 1, he skipped the 2017 Monaco Grand Prix to join the Andretti IndyCar team in the Indianapolis 500, where he led for nearly 30 laps, but his engine malfunctioned, leading to his coming in twenty-fourth. In 2018, driving for Toyota, he won the 24 Hours of Le Mans endurance race, and in 2019, he won both the 24 Hours of Daytona and the 24 Hours of Le Mans again, and won the FIA World Endurance Championship title for 2018 to 2019. In 2021, Alonso returned to

Formula 1 as a driver for Alpine (formerly Renault), and switched to Aston Martin for the 2023 season, during which he scored eight podiums!

Q: Which record-breaking driver is leaving his team for Ferrari in 2025?

A: Lewis Hamilton, seven-time World Champion, is reportedly leaving Mercedes to drive for Scuderia Ferrari for the 2025 season.

CHAPTER 4

PEDAL TO THE METAL

F1 CARS AND EQUIPMENT

Q: Are F1 cars street legal?

A: No, current Formula 1 cars are not street legal. They are missing a great many safety features required on street cars, they have open wheels, and they are far too fast and powerful to drive alongside cars on regular roads.

Q: What is the proper term for a Formula 1 car engine?

A: What we would call a "car engine" in Formula 1 is referred to as a "power unit." Since 2014, the power of Formula 1 cars is generated by both a gasoline engine and electrical generators, making them technically hybrids. These hybrid power units currently consist of the following main components:

- Internal combustion engine (ICE)—As of this writing, a 1.6-liter V6 gasoline-powered engine.

- Turbocharger (TC)—This component uses engine exhaust to spin a turbine that in turn runs a compressor, which results in more and higher-pressure air than a typical car's air compressor, funneling into the engine, increasing the gas engine's power and efficiency.

- Energy recovery system (ERS), which has the following main components:

  - Motor generator unit—Kinetic (MGU-K)—A device that captures energy from braking.

  - Motor generator unit—Heat (MGU-H)—A device that captures heat energy from turbocharging.

  - Control electronics (CE)—The component that converts the MGU energy for storage.

⮑ Energy store (ES)—The battery where the CE sends the energy it got from the MGUs for later use.

Additionally, since 2022, another component, the engine exhaust system (EX), is now also considered a part of the power unit, although they don't really power the vehicle. Like on a regular car, this expels the fumes generated by the gas burned by the engine.

Q: What manufacturers supply power units for F1 cars?

A: As of this writing, only four manufacturers supply Formula 1 power units: Ferrari, Mercedes, Renault, and Honda Red Bull Powertrains.

Q: What power unit changes are expected for F1 vehicles?

A: The FIA-mandated specs for Formula 1 power units are slated to change for the 2026 season to increase the utilization of electrical power and to run on fuel that is 100 percent sustainable.

Q: What are the power and weight differences between an F1 car and a road car?

A: A typical car that you can drive on the street is on average twice as heavy and a tenth to a third as powerful as a Formula 1 racing vehicle.

Q: What is the horsepower of a typical Formula 1 vehicle?

A: One unit of horsepower is the power it takes to move 550 pounds one foot in one second (and is a concept that originated from the time we used horses for transportation rather than cars). Typical modern road cars range between 100 and 300 horsepower. But modern Formula 1 vehicles run at a horsepower of around 1,000!

Q: How many revolutions per minute does an F1 engine reach?

A: Formula 1 car engines can run at around 15,000 revolutions per minute (rpm). By comparison, a typical road car is closer to 2,000 rpm.

Q: What is the fuel efficiency of an F1 vehicle?

A: Since Formula 1 cars now use hybrid technologies for power, their fuel efficiency has improved drastically over the years. The F1 cars of the 1960s burned around 195 kilograms per hour (around 51.5 gallons per hour), whereas modern F1 cars now use (and, in fact, are only allowed to use) a maximum of 100 kilograms per hour (around 26.4 gallons per hour). Although there are road cars with better fuel efficiency overall, they aren't being pushed at 200 miles an hour like F1 vehicles, making this a remarkable achievement. F1 vehicle fuel is also required to be at least 10 percent ethanol (called E10 fuel) and the industry is shooting for 100 percent sustainable fuel for the 2026 season.

Q: Can a Formula 1 team swap out power units for every race?

A: This used to be allowed. But there is now a limit on the number of power unit components that can be used over the course of a season, and exceeding it results in penalties. As of this writing, the limits are two energy stores, two control

electronics units, three ICE units, three turbochargers, three MGU-Ks, three MGU-Hs, and eight engine exhaust systems.

Q: What extra components were allowed during the 2023 season?

A: A last-minute change was made to the 2023 spring weekend rules. Therefore, the FIA allowed teams to use an extra ICE, TC, MGU-H, and MGU-K during the 2023 season.

Q: What material are modern F1 race car chassis made of?

A: The monocoque chassis of modern-day F1 race cars are made of carbon fiber. These replaced the previous fused-aluminum chassis (which had themselves replaced the steel spaceframe chassis of the original F1 cars). Read the next entry to learn more about this amazing material.

Q: What is carbon fiber?

A: Carbon fiber is a very strong but lightweight polymer first invented in the 1860s by English chemist and physicist Sir Joseph Wilson Swan for use as a lightbulb filament. In the 1950s and 1960s, the processes for producing and molding carbon fiber made it viable as a manufacturing material. It is basically extremely thin (5 to 10 microns thick) strands of carbon woven together. Carbon fiber is five times stronger than steel but one-third the weight. To make a chassis out of solid carbon fiber, sheets of the material (along with resin to bond them) are layered onto a mold of the required shape in a clean room and heated up under pressure in an autoclave to reduce their bulk and to cure them into their final hard and strong form.

Q: What typical buttons, knobs, and levers are on the steering wheel of a modern F1 car?

A: The steering wheels of F1 cars have a lot more controls on them than regular road car steering wheels, even in the computer age when we can control things like music streaming services from the wheel. In fact, F1 car steering wheels look like souped-up gaming controllers. This is mainly because an F1 driver is rarely, if ever, supposed to remove their hands from the steering wheel, as it takes a lot of focus and strength to keep the car on the track. There are buttons and knobs to change a number of car settings on the fly, a button to activate the drag reduction system (see page 79), a button to keep the car from going faster than the pit lane speed limit, a button to alert the pit crew of the car's imminent arrival, a button to mark a point in time the driver thinks the team should check the data, a button to shift into neutral, and two separate paddles for shifting down or up. These can and do change over time and from team to team, of course.

Q: What special hydration system do F1 cars have?

A: Drivers need to stay as hydrated as possible. The high temperatures generated by the cars causes drivers to sweat away several pounds during a race (see Chapter 6 for more details). The cars now include a system that allows drivers to drink from a tube attached to their helmets. The fluid is contained in a pouch in the car. When the driver gets out of the car, the tube automatically disconnects.

Q: What elements of an F1 car produce the downforce effect that keeps them on the track?

A: In the case of aerodynamics, form and function are often one and the same. Downforce (as defined in Chapter 1 and embellished upon in an entry on Chapter 6) is an effect of physics that is integral to certain types of racing, especially F1 racing. Cars are designed with the aerodynamic expertise once reserved for airplanes so that they harness the power of the air, although in reverse. With a plane, its wings and other aerodynamic elements provide lift, where the air, like it sounds, lifts the plane into the sky. An F1 car's aerodynamic elements cause it to be pushed toward the ground. The parts of the car that help harness this effect are the front and rear wings, Venturi tunnels on the underbelly of the car (named for Italian physicist Giovanni Battista Venturi; see Chapter 6 for more details on the science of the Venturi effect), and a diffuser at the rear of the vehicle. See Chapter 6 for more on the physics of downforce.

Q: What is the DRS on an F1 race car?

A: Drag reduction system (DRS) was introduced in Formula 1 racing in 2011. In this system, the rear wing of the car has a built-in flap. The driver can push a steering wheel button to open the flap to reduce drag and increase speed on straight segments of the track. While the flap is closed, the rear wing is essentially a sealed single curved piece that causes air to push the car down onto the track (downforce). When the flap is open, air goes through the wing rather than over it, decreasing drag. At the time of this writing, the DRS opening can be no more than 88mm (about 3.5 inches). DRS can increase the speed from around 6 to 12 miles per hour.

Q: Under what circumstances is a driver allowed to use DRS?

A: There are a few rules for when and under what circumstances a driver is allowed to use DRS to potentially overtake the driver ahead of them. DRS can only be activated in DRS zones along the circuit (stretches of track that are officially ruled safe for DRS use). In an actual race, there must be a car within one second of the driver who uses DRS. During practice and qualifying rounds, a driver can use DRS in any DRS zone whether there is anyone in front of them or not. DRS cannot be used at all during the first two laps of a race. It is also prohibited during the first two laps after a red flag or deployment of a safety car (see Chapters 1 and 5 for flag and safety car details). It can also be prohibited when there is a dangerous condition present on the track, like a wreck or wetness due to inclement weather.

Q: What circuits have the most and fewest DRS zones?

A: The Australian Grand Prix circuit at Albert Park has four DRS zones, the most of any circuit. The fewest is at Monaco, which has only one DRS zone. Although it has more than one straightaway, only one has been ruled safe enough for DRS.

Q: What is an ERS in an F1 car?

A: ERS stands for energy recovery system, which stores waste energy to give the car a boost later. A modern Formula 1 race car has two components that recover energy, consisting of two different MGUs. The MGU-K stores kinetic energy from the brakes and the MGU-H stores heat energy from the turbocharger. These components work alongside the control electronics that convert the recovered energy for storage and energy store, which is where the recovered energy is stored for later. All of the above comprise the ERS. This stored energy can be used later to give the car a temporary burst of speed. The braking ERS MGU-K is also sometimes referred to as the kinetic energy recovery system (KERS).

Q: What is an FHR system?

A: A Frontal Head Restraint (FHR) system is a safety device that prevents a driver's head and neck from being thrown forward forcefully during a crash. Head and Neck Support (HANS) and Hybrid are examples of an FHR, and the only two currently approved for use in F1.

Q: What is the difference between the HANS device and the Hybrid system?

A: Both are FHR systems (see above). HANS, which stands for Head and Neck Support, is a safety device that rests behind and is tethered to a driver's helmet and wraps around the neck to the front of the shoulders. It is fairly rigid and the early devices were quite heavy, although with new and better designs and materials, the weight has been brought down. The Hybrid serves the same purpose, but rather than a rigid piece that wraps around the head, it involves a device behind the head that is tethered to parts of the car with straps going in different directions to hold the driver's head in place, similarly to the way HANS works, but with less weight and more comfort.

Q: What materials are used to strengthen the helmets and cockpit sides?

A: The synthetic material Zylon is a polymer that is used to strengthen F1 helmets and cockpit sides. Like Kevlar, it is also used in bulletproof vests. The tensile strength of Zylon is 1.6

times higher than that of Kevlar. Both Zylon and Kevlar are used in F1 car construction.

Q: What are drivers required to wear while driving?

A: Whether in testing or practice, qualifying, or an actual Grand Prix race, F1 drivers are always required to wear all their racing gear anytime they are driving. Their gear includes a balaclava, a racing helmet, special gloves with biometric sensors to track health metrics, a fire-resistant racing suit, and racing boots.

Q: What fire-resistant material is used to make drivers' racing outfits?

A: Nomex is a fire-resistant synthetic material developed by DuPont that is used to coat drivers' outerwear, underwear, boots, and gloves. The protective gear undergoes testing to make sure it can withstand temperatures up to 800°F for more than 11 seconds.

Q: What material are the F1 cars' fuel cells made of?

A: The fuel cells are made of polyurethane and Kevlar so that in the event of a crash, they won't get punctured. This reduces the risk of fire or explosion. Kevlar is better known as the material used to make bulletproof vests.

Q: What safety features were introduced to Formula 1 as a result of injuries or fatalities?

A: Every wreck in F1 is thoroughly investigated to potentially improve the safety of the sport. Sometimes that comes in the

form of rule or circuit changes, and sometimes the result is new safety equipment.

- ➲ During a practice session at the 1959 Indianapolis 500 (which at the time was part of F1), Jerry Unser lost control of his car, hit a wall, and flipped down the track. The car burst into flames. He succumbed to his burns a couple of weeks later. As a result of this tragedy, the FIA made a rule that drivers must wear fire-resistant driving suits.

- ➲ During a practice round at a nonchampionship race in 1960, Henry O'Reilly "Harry" Schell died in a crash that flipped his car into a brick wall. He had been a proponent of roll bars (a strong piece of material usually in an arch shape behind the driver that goes up one side of the car, above the height of the driver, and down the other side to keep the driver from being crushed if the car flips over), and they were made mandatary in 1961 after his death.

- ➲ Following Jochen Rindt's fatal crash at the 1970 Italian Grand Prix at Monza (see Chapter 12 for details), six-point harnesses (a seat belt system with six straps attached to the car that wrap around the driver—two over the shoulders, two at the waist, and two at the crotch area—and buckle on the driver's frontside) were added.

- ➲ At a nonchampionship race at Brands Hatch in 1970, BRM driver Jo Siffert crashed when his car's suspension broke. He survived the impact but could not get out of the burning car and suffered smoke inhalation and died. In the investigation afterward, officials discovered that even if they had been able to get to him earlier, none of the fire extinguishers at the track were functional! The FIA added a rule that cars had to be fitted with their own fire extinguishers, and that helmets needed to have air piped in just in case of such an incident.

- Jackie Stewart had always been a staunch advocate for safety measures in motorsport, but after the horrific death of his friend and teammate, French driver François Cevert (see Chapter 12), he pushed even harder, and more people in the sport followed suit. Cevert's death likely led to faster adoption of many of the safety features that follow in this and the next entry.

- The number of gas tanks on a Formula 1 car was reduced to one in 1978 after Jo Siffert and Roger Williamson (1973 Dutch Grand Prix) died in car fires, and Niki Lauda was severely burned (1976 German Grand Prix).

- After Austrian driver Roland Ratzenberger and Brazilian driver Ayrton Senna were killed (both of head injuries) in the 1994 San Marino Grand Prix race weekend at the Imola circuit in Italy, the FIA became interested in the HANS device designed by Dr. Robert Hubbard in the 1980s after his race car–driving brother-in-law Jim Dowling lost a friend at Le Mans. It took a while, but the HANS device was made mandatory in F1 in 2003 (IndyCar and NASCAR made it mandatory in 2001 after the fatal crash of NASCAR's Dale Earnhardt).

- The two tragic fatalities weren't the only issues that plagued the 1994 Formula 1 race at Imola. Another injurious but nonfatal incident led to a pit stop speed limit of 80 kilometers (just under 50 miles) per hour, and drivers who break it can be fined or penalized.

⮑ Although helmets of some sort have been part of Formula 1 since the early 1950s, they have evolved and become far more protective over the decades. During the 2009 Hungarian Grand Prix, Felipe Massa was knocked unconscious and crashed when a spring flew off another vehicle and slammed into his helmet. He received a serious head injury that required multiple surgeries and the addition of a metal plate, which kept him out of racing for the rest of the season. As a result of the incident, a Zylon strip was added to the top of the visor for added protection. Later the helmet and visor were modified to make them safer, and the Zylon strip was removed.

⮑ The virtual safety car (VSC) was instituted after the crash at the 2014 Japanese Grand Prix that put Jules Bianchi in a coma and ultimately killed him nine months later (see Chapter 1 for the definition of the VSC and Chapter 12 for more details on the tragic accident).

⮑ The halo, a titanium structure that is attached to the car's chassis and circles above the driver's head, became part of Formula 1 and other motorsports in 2018 after multiple accidents that led to serious injury when large parts of wrecked cars flew into drivers' cockpits.

⮑ Safety panel improvements were made after Anthoine Hubert was killed in a multicar crash during the 2019 Formula 2 Belgian Grand Prix at Spa-Francorchamps.

⮑ More fire-resistant gloves were introduced after a crash at the 2020 Bahrain Grand Prix left driver Romain Grosjean with severely burned hands.

Q: What other safety-related changes have been introduced over the years?

A: There have been many additions and modifications to equipment to improve the safety of the sport. Some notable ones are:

⮑ In 1952, cork helmets.

⮑ In 1955, disc brakes.

⮑ In 1975, fire-resistant overalls required, and headrest and fire extinguishers added to cars.

⮑ In 1973, the safety car was introduced, although it wasn't made a permanent part of the sport until 1993.

⮑ In 1980, medical facilities at tracks.

⮑ In 1981, Kevlar-coated carbon fiber monocoques.

⮑ In 1986, medical helicopter.

⮑ In 1990, detachable steering wheels.

⮑ In 1994, fire-resistant suits worn by refueling crew.

⮑ In 1996, headrests to protect the driver's head and neck from the ill effects of high g-forces.

⮑ In 1997, an Accident Data Recorder to gather vital information used to improve the safety of the sport.

⮑ In 1999, wheel tethers.

⮑ In 2001, carbon fiber helmets.

⮑ In 2013, helmets for pit crews.

- In 2014, accelerometer earpieces to gather data on what the driver is going through.
- In 2015, Zylon chassis protection.
- In 2018, a 400-frame per second driver-facing camera and biometric gloves to track the driver's blood oxygen and pulse rates.

Q: What was the first Formula 1 car to have a full monocoque chassis?

A: The 1962 Lotus 25 was the first F1 race car with a full monocoque chassis (an earlier Jaguar had a partial one). The chassis was designed by Colin Chapman, cofounder of Lotus Engineering Ltd. and founder of team Lotus, which entered F1 racing in 1958. Chapman reportedly first sketched the design for the chassis on a restaurant napkin. Replacing the typical steel spaceframe of an F1 car at the time, the Lotus 25 had a chassis made of a single fused piece of aluminum. This new monocoque led to the driver looking like he was reclining more than the other drivers, leading to the Lotus 25 being dubbed the "bathtub." The chassis of a Formula 1 car is still often referred to as a tub because it kind of looks like one.

Q: What was the first Formula 1 car to have a carbon fiber monocoque?

A: The McLaren MP4/1, which made its debut in the Argentine Grand Prix in 1981 and was conceived by McLaren technical director John Barnard and British Aerospace aeronautical engineer Arthur Webb, was the first F1 racer to incorporate a carbon fiber monocoque. The monocoque was produced by US company Hercules Aerospace and the vehicle constructed by the McLaren team.

Q: Why can't an F1 race car accommodate different drivers on the same team in a race?

A: The seat of an F1 car is actually custom molded for its driver. To change drivers, the entire seat would have to be replaced.

Q: What car was only allowed to race once due to a major downforce advantage?

A: The Brabham BT46B was introduced in 1978 during the Swedish Grand Prix, driven by Niki Lauda racing for the Brabham team. Designer Gordon Murray had mounted a fan to the back of the car, ostensibly for cooling, but which pulled air from under the car, creating more downforce and allowing it to corner quickly. There was no rule against it. But it proved such an advantage that after Niki Lauda won the Swedish Grand Prix, the FIA immediately made a rule against the practice.

Q: What systems are controlled by hydraulics in an F1 car?

A: Hydraulics control 10 systems in a modern F1 vehicle, including:

- Brake-by-wire (where the brakes are controlled electronically rather than mechanically)
- Clutch
- Differential
- DRS system
- Gearshifts
- Inlet valves
- Power steering

➲ Reverse gear

➲ Throttle

➲ Turbo wastegate (a valve that releases excess exhaust to direct it away from the turbine to keep it spinning at a controlled speed)

Q: Where is the clutch located on an F1 car?

A: The clutch of an F1 car is located on the steering wheel.

Q: What sort of brakes does an F1 have?

A: The rear brakes of an F1 vehicle consist of hydraulic calipers that squeeze discs made of a carbon fiber composite material.

Q: How fast can a modern F1 car brake?

A: A modern Formula 1 race car can reach speeds in excess of 200 miles per hour. Astoundingly, they can go from breakneck speeds to a full stop within around four seconds!

Q: What controversial innovation did Mercedes implement in the 2020 season?

A: Mercedes debuted something they called dual access steering (DAS) during the 2020 season. It allowed the driver to push and pull the steering wheel of the car back and forth to change the tire position to be more toe-out to improve speed while cornering or less angled to improve tire temperature and grip on the straights. When other teams and commentators saw Mercedes drivers pulling and pushing the wheel into two different positions, it caused a bit of a kerfuffle. After an investigation, the FIA allowed Mercedes to continue using DAS for the 2020 season, but banned it thereafter.

Q: Why do many modern race car tires have no ridges?

A: The tires on normal cars have channels to funnel water out from underneath the tires to prevent hydroplaning in wet road conditions. But many F1 and other race car tires are totally slick. This allows for the entire surface of the tire to grip the ground and allow for heightened traction. But it also makes them terribly unsafe in the rain. There is therefore more than one type of racing tire. Read on to find out about F1 tire types.

Q: What are the different types of F1 tires?

A: There are actually multiple types of Formula 1 car tires made for different circumstances. The main categories are:

➲ Slicks—used in dry conditions

➲ Intermediates—used in combination wet/dry conditions

➲ Wets—used during wet weather when the cars are in danger of hydroplaning

There is only one of each intermediate and wet type tire each year. These are harder than the slicks and have ridges. But the slick tires come in multiple compounds of different softness levels. In 2023 there were six types of slick tire, numbered C0 (the hardest) through C5 (the softest). See Chapter 5 for the rules regarding which and how many of the tires are used on a given race weekend.

Q: What major change did F1 tire specs undergo in 2022?

A: For decades, Formula 1 tires were 13 inches, but in 2022, they were changed to 18 inches.

Q: What company supplies all Formula 1 tires through the 2024 season?

A: Since 2011, Italian company Pirelli has supplied all Formula 1 racing tires. Their contract to do so goes through 2024.

Q: What was the first rear-engine car to win an F1 race?

A: The earliest Formula 1 vehicles had their engines in front like most automobiles. The Cooper T43 was the first rear-engine vehicle to come in first in any F1 Grand Prix. Driver Stirling Moss achieved the feat at the 1958 Argentine Grand Prix. Rear-engine cars can be lighter, putting less wear on the tires, and one key to his victory was never stopping for tire replacement because he knew it would cost him several minutes (this was well before the FIA mandated that at least two tire compounds had to be used during each race except in the case of rain, which effectively mandated at least one pit stop during dry-weather races).

Q: What is a pit starter motor?

A: Until 2014, modern Formula 1 cars couldn't do something that road cars could—start on their own! The pit crew would have to connect a starter motor to start up the vehicle. And if the car stalled on the track, a starter motor would have to be driven out to it. Now drivers can restart their cars if they stall.

Q: What features are missing from Formula 1 cars that regular cars have?

A: One only has to look at the sleek, streamlined Formula 1 vehicles to see that they are not a typical car. But the differences go far beyond style. Here are several major differences between a Formula 1 car and a street-worthy car:

- F1 cars have no front or rear bumpers. Instead, they have wings designed with aerodynamics in mind. But as a result, parts of the car do not fare well during crashes.

- The wheels and tires of a Formula 1 car are not covered by the rest of the car. They are out in the open on full display.

- F1 cars are single-seater vehicles. They have one seat in the cockpit right in the middle of the vehicle, and this cockpit is a very tight space with only room for the driver and vital equipment. The driver has to remove the steering wheel to get out of the car.

- They are lighter than regular cars because they are missing a lot of the safety features required for street-worthy cars, and because many of their parts are made from lightweight materials like carbon fiber.

- Most of the controls that would normally be elsewhere, like the clutch, are on the steering wheel of a Formula 1 vehicle, along with lots of controls that regular cars do not have, like DRS (no need for drag reduction going down the interstate).

Q: What does the position of the brake pedal mean for F1 drivers versus regular road drivers?

A: Most regular drivers are taught to both brake and accelerate with their right foot for safety reasons (hitting both at the same time is not a great idea). But due to the tightness and configuration of the cockpit of a Formula 1 car, the driver must use their left foot to hit the brake pedal and right to hit the gas pedal.

Q: Why are the tires heated before being put onto an F1 car at a pit stop?

A: During every race, an F1 driver has to pull into the pit stop at least once to have the car's tires changed. The tires the pit crew put onto the car (usually within a couple of seconds) are preheated to improve grip.

Q: What is dyno testing?

A: Dyno testing is common throughout the automotive industry. During this testing, a car, or even just a car engine, are hooked up to a device called a dynamometer, which determines the horsepower of a car by measuring how many revolutions per minute (RPMs) the engine is running.

Q: When can F1 teams test their vehicles?

A: Formula 1 teams are allowed to factory test their vehicles all the way up to the beginning of an F1 season, but once the season starts, they cannot test the vehicles that are being used in competition. At that point they have to switch to testing via simulator runs. Read on to find out more about simulators and other testing tools.

Q: What equipment do drivers use to practice when they aren't in a car?

A: In the early days of F1 racing, and racing in general, the only way to learn how to do it was to hop in a car and do it. But now, Formula 1 drivers (including the Grand Prix racers, reserve drivers, and test drivers) log lots of hours in simulators that resemble video games, using controls much like the ones in the Formula 1 vehicles.

Q: What driver lost valuable pit stop time at the 2016 Monaco Grand Prix when his tires were not ready at a pit stop?

A: During the 2016 Monaco Grand Prix, Red Bull Racing driver Daniel Ricciardo took pole position and led the race in the beginning, only dropping behind Lewis Hamilton after pitting for intermediate tires due to track conditions. At Monaco, the pit wall staff is on top of the garage and can't see what's going on in the garage (unlike most circuits where they are across from their garages). In the Red Bull Racing garage, the pit crew had prepped soft tires, but the team decided on the fly to switch him to a set of super-soft tires that had been used briefly during qualifying, an order that was called down to the garage crew. The tires they called for were at the back of the garage, which is small and cramped at that circuit, and the crew couldn't get them out in time for Ricciardo's arrival at the pit. The delay made the pit stop go over by about 10 seconds. The delay quite possibly cost him first place, but Ricciardo still managed to come in second in the race despite the long pit stop.

Q: When did Red Bull Racing stop using Renault engines?

A: Since the Red Bull Racing team is run by an energy drink company, not a car manufacturer, they have to source their equipment from others. They used Renault engines from 2007 to 2018. During the 2018 season, the team made a deal with Honda to supply their engines for their future F1 cars starting in 2019. And due to Honda's upcoming withdrawal from the sport, Red Bull Racing will use Ford power units starting in 2026.

Q: How many gears does a modern F1 car have?

A: A typical road car has six or seven gears, but a Formula 1 vehicle has nine: eight forward gears plus reverse. And they aren't shifted via a gear stick to the side of the driver. They are shifted electronically via control paddles on the steering wheel that send signals to the F1 car's computer. Electronic shifting is much faster than manual shifting, which keeps the car from losing speed during shifts. And the controls allow the driver to keep their hands on the steering wheel.

Q: Why do F1 cars sometimes throw sparks behind them?

A: Sometimes cars do something called "bottoming," where the bottom of the chassis hits the racetrack. It can slow a driver down. In 2015, titanium skid blocks were added to the cars that throw sparks when they hit the ground.

Q: What item made of wood is required on all F1 vehicles?

A: An item called a "plank" is required on all Formula 1 cars. It is a strip of wood that runs lengthwise on the underside of the car to keep it from completely bottoming out. It was added as one of many features implemented after the terrible fatalities and injuries at the 1994 Grand Prix at Imola (see Chapter 12) to slow the cars down and make Formula 1 safer. With the plank, the cars can't be built too low, which decreases downforce. The skid blocks (mentioned above) help prevent wear on the plank. If the plank is worn down too much after a race, the driver can actually be disqualified (see Chapter 3 for two such driver disqualifications in one race that led to another driver setting a record with only one point).

Q: What are gremlins in F1?

A: Gremlins are the same in F1 as they are in all things mechanical: an anthropomorphic representation of things going wrong in the works; in this case, with a Formula 1 car.

Q: What is the setup of a car?

A: "Setup" refers to a set of parameters that can be adjusted on a car based on driver preferences and driving style, weather conditions, the traits of a circuit, and other factors. The driver and race engineer typically get together and make choices on the setup parameters for the car before each Grand Prix after checking out the circuit. Things like the position of the wings or the stiffness of the suspension can be adjusted as needed.

CHAPTER 5

FAST TRACK
F1 CIRCUITS AND COMPETITIONS

Q: What and when is pre-season practice?

A: Pre-season practice sessions are just three days that lately take place in Bahrain just before the start of the Formula 1 season. It is the first chance drivers get to try out the new iterations of their teams' cars.

Q: What is the typical format of a Formula 1 Grand Prix?

A: A Formula 1 Grand Prix takes place over three days (Friday through Sunday) and in recent history has usually consisted of three practice rounds (two on Friday and one on Saturday), qualifying rounds (Q1, Q2, and Q3) on Saturday, and the actual Grand Prix race on Sunday. Practice is what it sounds like it is, and qualifying results determine the drivers' starting positions in the Sunday race (with all hoping for the coveted pole position). However, changes have been thrown into some (but not all) of the Grand Prix weekends since 2021 in the form of Sprint Weekends (read on to find out more).

Q: What is an F1 Sprint weekend?

A: In 2021, Formula 1 introduced the F1 Sprint, which added a couple of elements to a Grand Prix race weekend to make things more exciting. Rather than practice, qualifying, and the race, the weekend consists of practice and qualifying on Friday, a Sprint Shootout and Sprint on Saturday, and the Grand Prix race on Sunday as usual. The Sprint Shootout is a qualifying round for the Sprint. The Sprint is a 30-minute, 100-km (62-mile) race. The Sprint results on Saturday don't have any bearing on the Sunday GP starting positions, but they can garner points for the drivers and teams.

Q: How many laps is a typical F1 race?

A: In the early days of the sport, an F1 race could have as many as 200 laps, when the Indianapolis Motor Speedway was one of the F1 championship circuits. But Formula 1 races do not have a set number of laps. All but the Monaco circuit have a set distance of 305 km (around 190 miles). The Monaco circuit is 260 km (or around 161 miles). The drivers have to drive at slower speeds in Monaco, so the distance is shorter to keep the race time reasonable. The number of laps is however many it takes to reach at least the minimum race distance, and it varies by circuit. Current circuit lap numbers range from a little over 40 to a little less than 80.

Q: How many teams does the FIA allow to compete in Formula 1?

A: Currently, 10 Formula 1 teams are approved to compete in Formula 1 by the FIA, but FIA rules allow for up to 12 teams. Any team that wants to join has to go through a rigorous vetting process and be approved by both the FIA and the Formula 1 organization to be added to a new season. At least one new team is vying for a spot for 2026 (see Chapter 3 for details of this potential new contender).

Q: Which Formula 1 racetrack was originally a test track for an automaker's regular vehicles?

A: Suzuka International Racing Course in Suzuka, Mie Prefecture, Japan, began as a test track for car manufacturer Honda.

Q: What is the highest speed Formula 1 circuit?

A: The highest speed track at the time of this writing is the Autodromo Nazionale di Monza circuit in Milan, Italy, which has been used for Formula 1 championships since the official beginning of the series in 1950 (see Chapter 2). The fastest lap in Formula 1 history thus far was set at Monza by Juan Pablo Montoya in 2004 during a practice round, at 260.6 kilometers (roughly 161.9 miles) per hour. Monza is sometimes called the "Temple of Speed." The next-fastest current circuits are Jeddah and Silverstone.

Q: What is the fastest street circuit?

A: While Monza is the fastest of all the circuits, it is a permanent track. The fastest overall street circuit (those that use public streets) is the Jeddah Corniche Circuit in Saudi Arabia, which hosted its first Grand Prix in 2021.

Q: What continent currently doesn't host any F1 Grands Prix?

A: Currently, none of the countries on the African continent have hosted a Formula 1 Grand Prix since the 1993 South African Grand Prix at the Kyalami Circuit near Johannesburg. Plans were in the works to resume this competition in 2024, but they have been put on hold due to accusations that the country has supplied arms to Russia to aid in their invasion of Ukraine.

Q: What are the most important flags and their meanings in F1?

A: The following are several important flags and their meanings:

- White flag—This flag warns that there is a slow-moving car on the track.

- Blue flag—The blue flag is waved at backmarker cars when lead cars are approaching. It is to warn the driver to get out of the way of faster cars safely.

- Yellow flag—This flag indicates danger on or near the track. Whether it is held still, waved, or double-waved also indicates the level of the danger.

- Yellow with red stripes—This flag indicates that the track is slick, usually due to the presence of oil or water.

- Green flag—Following a yellow flag, a green flag indicates that the danger is no longer present on the track.

- Red flag—This flag indicates that the race has been terminated, often due to bad weather conditions or a serious accident. All drivers must return to their respective pits.

- Black flag—This flag indicates that the driver has been disqualified due to a rule infringement and must return to the pit stop and cease driving. It is displayed along with the driver's number.

- Black flag with orange circle in the middle—This flag indicates that the driver must return to the pit due to a dangerous mechanical issue with their car.

- Half-black, half-white flag on either side of the diagonal—This flag is a warning to a driver that they are doing something wrong and they are in danger of getting a penalty if they continue.

➲ Checkered flag—Probably the most recognized flag in racing, the black and white checkered flag is waved at the finish line at the end of the race.

Flags are waved by marshals at their booths on the track. Some also appear on the driver's cockpit display panels so that they won't be missed.

Q: What Grand Prix holds the record for most red flags deployed during the race?

A: During the 2023 season Australian Grand Prix at Melbourne, red flags had to be deployed three times due to incidents that scattered debris on the track. The third red flag happened on the next-to-the-last lap of the race, resulting in the race being finished with the virtual safety car deployed.

Q: What is the purpose of a chicane?

A: A chicane is a series of corners on the circuit that are close together and change direction at least twice, often forming a sort of S-shaped curve in the track. Chicanes are designed to slow the cars down for safety.

Q: Where did the word "chicane" come from?

A: Chicane (as defined above) has the same root at the word chicanery, which means trickery. Both come from the Middle French word chicaner, which means "to quibble."

Q: What features of a circuit often have colorful names?

A: You might hear an F1 circuit's corners referred to by their number (Turn 1, Turn 2, etc.), but you might also hear them referred to by name. The corners, chicanes, and some of the straights at racetracks tend to have unique names. They might be named for drivers, like the Schumacher turn at the Bahrain International Circuit or the Mansell turn at Mexico's Autodromo Hermanos Rodriguez, or named for the nearby scenery, like the Beau Rivage ("beautiful coastline") and Casino Square (which is near a casino) corners at Monaco or the Eau Rouge at Spa-Francorchamps (named for the red iron-heavy water that flows underneath a bridge at the corner). Some are named for their shapes or sizes, like The Loop at Silverstone, Hairpin at Monaco, and 130R at Suzuka (the turn's metric radius). Others are named for things that used to be at or near the site of the circuit, like Abbey (for the ruins of Luffield Abbey) and Wellington Straight (named for the bombers that used to reside at the former airfield turned racing circuit). These are but a few of many colorful names, all with their own stories.

Q: What sort of barriers and landscaping are in place to minimize danger of crashes?

A: Accidents will happen, especially when a car is going 100 to 200 mph. In the old days, the barriers and runoff areas of circuits were usually just the natural landscape around the track, or things like hay bales (which were banned in 1967) and simple fences. A lot of areas had no barriers whatsoever between the cars and the race crew and even spectators, leading to preventable injuries and fatalities.

To curtail serious injury to racers and spectators alike when a car skids off the track or crashes, every circuit now includes lots of features to minimize the chance of disaster. These include things like asphalt paving, gravel traps, and barriers. Barriers might be made of tires with inserts or new TechPro blocks.

These barriers absorb more of the impact of a crash than, say, a concrete wall, protecting the driver, but they still prevent cars and debris from flying in the stands or pits much better than the old hay bales. The TechPro barrier blocks are made of hollow polyethylene that can be connected with straps to form walls of different shapes and sizes. Another fairly modern circuit feature is rumble strips, which line the turns on most tracks and have ridges that cause a noise when tires run over them.

Q: How is a driver penalized for rule infractions?

A: When a driver is deemed to have broken a rule, there are several possible penalties they might be given.

- Time penalty: 5- or 10-second penalties require the driver to either stay in a pit stop for an extra 5 or 10 seconds, or, if they don't have to make a pit stop, the seconds are added to the driver's overall time at the end of the race.

- Drive-through penalty: Requires them to drive through the pit lane at a reduced speed of 60 kph (37 mph) before rejoining the race at full speed.

- Stop-and-go penalty: Requires the driver to pull into the pit lane and stop for a set number of seconds without receiving any pit-crew assistance before resuming the race.

- Black flag penalty: The most severe race-time penalty. As mentioned in the flag entry, this means that the driver has been disqualified and must pull into a pit stop and quit the race.

Q: What do DNS, DNQ, and DNF mean in F1?

A: DNS means "did not start." DNQ means "did not qualify." And DNF means "did not finish." All refer to the status of drivers for a particular race.

Q: What is the 107 percent rule in F1?

A: The 107 percent rule stipulates that any driver who does not complete a lap within at least 107 percent of the fastest lap in the first qualifying session cannot compete. The rule was instituted in 1996, revoked in 2002, and reinstituted in 2011, and its aim is to make sure everyone is driving close to the same speeds for safety reasons. Exceptions can be made, for instance if a driver achieved the appropriate lap time during practice or if mechanical failure or weather conditions caused the longer lap times during qualifying. One example where this rule could have been invoked, but thankfully for the team and driver was waived, was during the 2023 Saudia Arabia Grand Prix. The fastest lap time in Q1 was set by Max Verstappen at 1:28.761. Logan Sargeant had a 1:29:721 lap time in Q1, which was within 107 percent of Verstappen's time, but because he crossed the white painted lines between the track and pit entry during the lap, he was penalized by having that time deleted. But during practice, Sargeant had lap times between 1:30.035 and 1:31.922, so the marshals took that into consideration and allowed him to race.

Q: What are the F1 rules about cars passing other cars?

A: F1 guidelines for passing center on an idea called the "right to space." But how that is interpreted in actual races as to whether "right to space" has been violated is up to the stewards. Cars cannot pass each other during a formation lap or when the safety car is out or activated. If a driver has their front wheel in front of another driver's back wheel on the inside of a corner, they are allowed to overtake the front car, but on an outside corner, they have to be driving alongside each other. A driver is allowed to move once to stop a car behind them from overtaking, but weaving back and forth is against the rules. And when the marshals have deployed a blue flag at a backmarker car that is about to be lapped, that car must move out of the way of the approaching faster car.

Q: What was the first Brazilian circuit race to be a part of the F1 world championship?

A: The 1973 Brazilian Grand Prix at Interlagos was the first to be a part of a Formula 1 world championship. Brazilian driver Emerson Fittipaldi of team Lotus came in first during both the 1973 and 1974 Brazilian Grands Prix, and Brazilian driver Carlos Pace took first during the 1975 Grand Prix. The circuit was renamed the Autodromo Jose Carlos Pace in 1985.

Q: What circuits held Formula 1 Grands Prix during the inaugural season of the sport?

A: Formula 1 became an official world championship motorsport in 1950 (see Chapter 2). Whereas now there are over 20 Grands Prix per year in Formula 1, the inaugural season only had seven. The circuits and their Grands Prix during the very first season of Formula 1 were:

- ⮑ Silverstone Circuit—British Grand Prix
- ⮑ Circuit de Monaco—Grand Prix de Monaco
- ⮑ Indianapolis Motor Speedway—Indianapolis Grand Prix

- Circuit Bremgarten—Switzerland Grand Prix

- Circuit de Spa-Francorchamps—Belgian Grand Prix

- Circuit de Reims-Gueux—French Grand Prix

- Autodromo Nazionale di Monza—Italian Grand Prix

Q: What manufacturer's vehicles were used more than any other individual make during the 1950 Formula 1 World Championship Grand Prix?

A: The rules regarding cars and teams were not nearly as stringent in the beginning as they have been since the Concorde Agreement (see Chapter 8). Early on, teams didn't have to enter every single race, most of the rules had to do with the capacity of the car's engines and a couple of basic safety features, and the same cars didn't have to be used for the whole season. There were even F1 races that weren't part of the official Formula 1 World Championship. The cars driven during the 1950 World Championship races included one model of Cooper, one of Watson, two models of Alfa Romeo, three Kurtis Kraft models, three Maserati models, three Talbot-Lago models, and five models of Ferrari. Ferrari was the most represented manufacturer in the first season of the Formula 1 World Championship.

Q: Why has the Grand Prix at Imola, Italy, only been called the Italian Grand Prix once?

A: There was already an Italian Grand Prix at Monza in Italy (mentioned in previous entries), which was among the first Formula 1 World Championship competitions held during the inaugural 1950 season. A Formula 1–worthy circuit opened at Imola, Italy, in 1953. It held its first Formula 1 race in 1963, but it was a nonchampionship race. In 1980, Imola hosted the Italian Grand Prix instead of Monza. But multiple Grands Prix were not allowed to have the same name. So starting in 1981, Grands Prix held at Imola took on the name San Marino Grand Prix and the ones at Monza kept the moniker Italian Grand Prix. The San Marino Grand Prix was held up until 2006. There were no Formula 1 Grands Prix at Imola from then until 2020, when their event was renamed once again to the Emilia Romagna Grand Prix.

What Formula 1 circuits run counterclockwise?

Most Formula 1 circuits are driven clockwise (the same direction the hands on a clock go). But a few are raced counterclockwise (sometimes called anticlockwise). The circuits that run counterclockwise are:

- Autodromo Enzo e Dino Ferrari at Imola, Italy
- Autodromo Jose Carlos Pace (aka Interlagos) in Sao Paulo, Brazil
- Circuit of the Americas in Austin, Texas

How truncated was the 2020 season due to the COVID-19 outbreak?

The 2020 Formula 1 season was set to begin in Melbourne, Australia, in March, right around the time the COVID-19 virus outbreak was becoming a worldwide concern. All the teams showed up in Melbourne for the Australian Grand Prix, but very soon after, before practice rounds had even started, at least two people on the McLaren team were showing symptoms. In the ranks of the Formula 1 teams and officials, there was a split on whether to hold the Grand Prix or cancel. World Champion driver Lewis Hamilton was one of the people dismayed that they were even trying to hold the Grand Prix under the circumstances, and when asked by reporters why he thought it was going forward, he famously said, "Cash is king." When a McLaren mechanic tested positive for COVID-19, the Grand Prix weekend was canceled, and everyone was sent home.

Q: What circuits held Formula 1 competitions in 2023?

A: The circuits that hold F1 races change from time to time. These were the Formula 1 Grands Prix in 2023:

- Gulf Air Bahrain Grand Prix at the Bahrain International Circuit in Sakhir, Bahrain, March 3 to 5
- STC Saudi Arabian Grand Prix at the Jeddah Corniche Circuit in Jeddah, Saudi Arabia, March 17 to 19
- Rolex Australian Grand Prix at the Melbourne Grand Prix in Melbourne, Australia, March 31 to April 2
- Azerbaijan Grand Prix at the Baku City Circuit in Baku, Azerbaijan, April 28 to 30
- Crypto.com Miami Grand Prix at the Miami International Autodrome in Miami, Florida, USA, May 5 to 7
- Grand Prix de Monaco at the Circuit de Monaco in Monte Carlo and La Condamine, Monaco, May 26 to 28
- AWS Gran Premio de España at the Circuit de Barcelona-Catalunya in Barcelona, Spain, June 2 to 4
- Pirelli Grand Prix du Canada at the Circuit Gilles-Villeneuve in Montreal, Quebec, Canada, June 16 to 18
- Rolex Grosser Preis von Osterreich at the Red Bull Ring in Spielberg, Austria, June 30 to July 2

- Aramco British Grand Prix at the Silverstone Circuit in Silverstone, England, July 7 to 9

- Qatar Airways Hungarian Grand Prix at the Hungaroring in Budapest, Hungary, July 21 to 23

- MSC Cruises Belgian Grand Prix at the Circuit de Spa-Francorchamps in Spa, Belgium, July 28 to 30

- Heineken Dutch Grand Prix at the Circuit Zandvoort in Zandvoort, Netherlands, August 25 to 27

- Pirelli Gran Premio d'Italia at the Autodromo Nazionale di Monza in Monza, Italy, September 1 to 3

- Singapore Airlines Singapore Grand Prix at the Marina Bay Street Circuit in Marina Bay, Singapore, September 15 to 17

- Lenovo Japanese Grand Prix at the Suzuka International Racing Course in Suzuka, Mie Prefecture, Japan, September 22 to 24

- Qatar Airways Qatar Grand Prix at the Lusail International Circuit in Lusail, Qatar, October 6 to 8

- Lenovo United States Grand Prix in the Circuit of the Americas in Austin, Texas, October 20 to 22

- Gran Premio de la Ciudad de Mexico at the Autodromo Hermanos Rodriguez in Mexico City, Mexico, October 27 to 29

- Rolex Grande Premio de Sao Paulo at the Autodromo Jose Carlos Pace (aka Interlagos) in Sao Paulo, Brazil, November 3 to 5

- Heineken Silver Las Vegas Grand Prix at the Las Vegas Strip Circuit in Las Vegas, Nevada, November 16 to 18

➦ Etihad Airways Abu Dhabi Grand Prix at the Yas Marina Circuit in Yas Island, Abu Dhabi, November 24 to 26

Another, the Qatar Airways Gran Premio Del Made In Italy e Dell, Emilia-Romagna at the Autodromo Enzo e Dino Ferrari in Imola, Italy, was scheduled for May 19 through 21, but was canceled due to flooding.

Q: What changes to the F1 schedule are slated in 2024?

A: The schedule has been shuffled around a bit in 2024 but includes the same locations as 2023 (including the previously canceled Gran Premio Del Made In Italy) plus an additional Lenovo Chinese Grand Prix at the Shanghai International Circuit in China.

Q: What was the Red Bull Ring originally called?

A: The Osterreichring was built in Spielberg, Austria, in 1969 as a replacement for the bumpy and unpopular Zeltweg airfield circuit. Osterreichring's original layout was used for Formula 1 Grands Prix from 1970 to 1987 but was still used for motorbike racing for a while. The circuit was remodeled considerably from 1995 through 1996 into the length and shape that it is today (which is wider and shorter than the original circuit). After this redesign, it was redubbed the A1-Ring. It fell into disuse after the 2003 Grand Prix, after which plans were hatched for a new remodel to make the circuit more modern. The project was completed in 2011 and the circuit was once again renamed, this time to the Red Bull Ring. Formula 1 races were once again raced at this circuit in Spielberg, Austria, starting in 2014.

ℚ? What large object was added to the middle of the Red Bull Ring?

🅐? In 2012, construction of a 68-ton steel bull sculpture, leaping underneath an arch, was completed. The rust-red beast with gold-colored horns stands about 17.2 meters (around 56 feet, 5 inches) tall upon a foundation of steel and concrete.

ℚ? What is the Red Bull Wing at the Red Bull Ring circuit?

🅐? The Red Bull Wing is a building at the site of the Red Bull Ring in Spielberg, Austria, that is designed to look somewhat like a Formula 1 racing car wing. It includes a welcome center, a fan shop, and a wing café.

ℚ? What does it mean when a track or section of track is described as "Mickey Mouse"?

🅐? A Mickey Mouse track or Mickey Mouse curb or chicane is very twisty and makes the drivers have to slow way down.

ℚ? What circuit was built on a man-made island?

🅐? The Circuit Guilles-Villeneuve, formerly the Île Notre-Dame, in Montreal, Canada, is the resurrection of the roads on an island created on the St. Lawrence River for the Expo 67 World's Fair in 1967, called Notre Dame Island. It hosted its first Grand Prix in 1978. In 1982, the circuit was renamed for Formula 1 Canadian driver Gilles Villeneuve, who got his first win at the location's inaugural Canadian Grand Prix.

ⓔ? What new Spanish circuit is being added in 2026?

Ⓐ? A new circuit has been announced to host the 2026 Spanish Grand Prix. It will be located in Madrid, and the current plans are for the track to circle much of the IFEMA Madrid exhibition center and extend into the sports arena area across the street. The circuit will be a hybrid of existing public roads and newly built permanent racetrack.

ⓔ? Who won the first Bahrain Grand Prix?

Ⓐ? The first Bahrain Grand Prix took place at the newly built Bahrain International Circuit in 2004. Ferrari driver Michael Schumacher took first, followed by his teammate Rubens Barrichello in second and Williams driver Juan Pablo Montoya in third.

ⓔ? Which circuits are temporary tracks?

Ⓐ? In F1, some circuits are permanent structures purpose-built for only racing, some are temporarily blocked off sections of streets and roads (either public or in places like sports complexes), and some are a combination. The current tracks that are built up and then broken down for each Grand Prix include:

- The Circuit de Monaco in Monte Carlo, Monaco
- The Jeddah Corniche Circuit in Jeddah, Saudi Arabia
- The Melbourne Grand Prix Circuit in Melbourne, Australia
- The Baku City Circuit in Baku, Azerbaijan
- The Miami International Autodrome in Miami, Florida
- The Las Vegas Strip Circuit in Las Vegas, Nevada

Q: What location has hosted the most Grands Prix?

A: The country of Italy has hosted 105 Grands Prix, making it the only one to break 100. The majority have been held at Monza, followed by Imola, with two one-off events at Pescara in 1957 and Mugello in 2020 (due to the pandemic).

Q: Which circuit is the newest street circuit?

A: The Baku City Circuit is a circuit along the shoreline and through the streets of the city of Baku, Azerbaijan. It was added to the Formula 1 calendar in 2016, making it the newest street circuit as of this writing.

Q: What is the shortest circuit in Formula 1?

A: The shortest Formula 1 circuit is the Circuit de Monaco, a city street circuit that is only 3.337 km (2.074 miles) long.

Q: What circuit has the longest track?

A: The Circuit de Spa-Francorchamps is 7.004 km (4.352 miles), making it the longest in total track length of the Formula 1 circuits.

Q: What track has the longest straight in Formula 1?

A: The Baku City Circuit in Azerbaijan has a 2.2-kilometer-long (1.367-mile-long) straight along Baku's shoreline of the Caspian Sea. It is currently the longest straight of the Formula 1 circuits and is known for drivers reaching speeds of up to 350 kilometers (or around 217 miles) per hour.

Q: What driver went airborne during the 1997 Austrian Grand Prix?

A: During the 1997 Austrian Grand Prix at the A1-Ring (now the Red Bull Ring), Benetton driver Jean Alesi and Ferrari driver Eddie Irvine went into and came out of a curve side by side until Alesi's vehicle caught and drove up Irvine's and became fully airborne for a moment before crashing back down to the track. Alesi was immediately out of the race in a gravel trap, and Irvine drove for a bit longer until he had to stop due to the damage to his car. Fortunately, no one was physically injured, although there were some psychic wounds. Alesi believed Irvine's driving to be at fault, but the stewards only investigated Alesi. He was exonerated by the FIA, which found no one at fault and deemed it an unfortunate driving incident.

Q: Which F1 circuit was built for the Olympics?

A: The Circuit de Barcelona-Catalunya in Spain was built for the 1992 Olympics.

Q: In what Grand Prix were no drivers able to pass each other?

A: The Circuit de Monaco is a street circuit well known for its narrow streets and the difficulty of passing. In fact during the Monaco Grand Prix in 2003, no driver managed to pass any other driver! They all placed in the positions where they started the race.

Q: What current Formula 1 circuit has also hosted Super Bowls?

A: The temporary Miami International Autodrome circuit is located in and around the Hard Rock Stadium compound in

Miami, Florida, which is headquarters of the Miami Dolphins and has hosted six Super Bowl events.

Q: What was the F1 race with the longest duration?

A: During the 2011 Canadian Grand Prix, there was a two-hour rain delay that caused the race to last around four hours and four minutes.

Q: What is the FIA-mandated maximum race duration?

A: There was no maximum before 2011, when the FIA added a rule that an F1 race could not last more than four hours. In 2021, this cap was reduced to three hours.

Q: How do drivers score points in a race?

A: The first ten drivers to cross the finish line (barring penalties) are the ones who score points in a race. These are the points awarded for a completed regular full-length Grand Prix race:

- 1st place—25 points
- 2nd place—18 points
- 3rd place—15 points
- 4th place—12 points
- 5th place—10 points
- 6th place—8 points
- 7th place—6 points
- 8th place—4 points
- 9th place—2 points
- 10th place—1 point

If one of the top ten drivers also has the fastest lap during the race, they get an extra point.

Q: Are points awarded for a race that ends sooner than it is supposed to?

A: The answer is yes, provided that the head driver has completed at least two laps. But the drivers don't get full points unless over 75 percent of the race distance was completed before the race was ended. And at less than 50 percent, fewer drivers get points. Here are the point breakdowns for the three other tiers of race completion:

➲ 50 to 75 percent completion:

first place—19 points; second place—14 points; third place—12 points; fourth place—9 points; fifth place—8 points; sixth place—6 points; seventh place—5 points; eighth place—3 points; ninth place—2 points; tenth place—1 point

➲ 25 to 50 percent completion:

first place—13 points; second place—10 points; third place—8 points; fourth place—6 points; fifth place—5 points; sixth place—4 points; seventh place—3 points; eighth place—2 points; ninth place—1 point

➲ At least two laps at regular speed (nonsafety car) from the leader to 25 percent completion:

first place—6 points; second place—4 points; third place—3 points; fourth place—2 points; fifth place—1 point

Q: What points are awarded for Sprints?

A: These newer, shorter races called Sprints award points to the top eight drivers as follows:

- First place—8 points
- Second place—7 points
- Third place—6 points
- Fourth place—5 points
- Fifth place—4 points
- Sixth place—3 points
- Seventh place—2 points
- Eighth place—1 point

Q: How do teams score points in a race?

A: Each team's points for the race are the tally of the points both their drivers scored during the race.

Q: How is a season's Drivers' World Champion picked?

A: Simply put, the driver who racked up the most points during the season becomes that year's Drivers' World Champion.

Q: How is the Constructors' World Champion chosen?

A: In the case of the Constructor Championship, the team whose drivers' points added together amount to the highest score becomes the Constructors' World Champion for the year.

Q: What natural occurrence aided by human error stymied the 2009 Malaysian Grand Prix?

A: The Malaysian Grand Prix at the Sepang International Circuit usually took place earlier in the day, but in 2009 the FIA decided to move it to late afternoon—a time it typically rained in the area. On race day April 5, 2009, nature did not disappoint (or did, in the case of foiling F1). In lap 5, it wasn't raining yet, but there was audible thunder. Dark clouds began to cover the sky. In lap 18, Ferrari driver Raikkonen was the first to pit for wet tires. Nineteen laps into the race, it began to rain. Around lap 30, lightning struck the commentators' box! It got heavier

and heavier until around lap 31, when drivers were complaining of lack of visibility, and worse, hydroplaning off the track! The safety car was deployed. Not long after, the red flag went up. The drivers were forced to stop on the grid and wait to see whether they would be able to resume the race. They were out for a while and their staff came out to tend to them—including holding umbrellas over them. Ultimately, the race was called, and the official final positions were based on the drivers' spots on the previous lap, and the top eight were awarded half the usual points. Jenson Button came in first followed by Nick Heidfeld in second and Timo Glock in third. And, of course, future race times were set back to a dryer time of day.

Q: What driver yelled for a white visor during the 2009 Malaysian Grand Prix downpour?

A: At the 2009 Malaysian Grand Prix, while the drivers were all stuck on the grid waiting to see if the race would restart during a red flag caused by heavy rain, Ferrari driver Felipe Massa famously demanded a white visor be brought to him or otherwise he wouldn't be able to see. A teammate responded for him to "keep cool" and that the visor was coming. The clip went viral. See Chapter 4 for a not-so-amusing helmet- and visor-related incident with Massa that occurred later at the 2009 Hungarian Grand Prix.

Q: What Grands Prix have had to be canceled due to political unrest?

A: The 2011 Bahrain Grand Prix was canceled due to anti-government, pro-democracy protests breaking out in the country in February, during which at least nine protestors were killed. The Bahrain Grand Prix resumed the next year. And the 2022 VTB

Russian Grand Prix was canceled by Formula 1 and hasn't been held since (at the time of this writing) due to Russia's invasion of Ukraine in February 2022.

Q: What 2023 Grand Prix saw multiple drivers get sick from the heat?

A: The 2023 Qatar Grand Prix took place during extreme heat. Multiple drivers took ill on race day. The problem was so bad that it prompted a rule change for 2024. The FIA will allow the cars to include an air shaft into the cockpit to help cool the drivers. And the Grand Prix at that location was moved to later in the year when the temperatures are cooler.

Q: What Formula 1 Grand Prix races take place at night?

A: Most Formula 1 races take place during broad daylight. In fact, they all were until the inaugural Singapore Grand Prix in 2008. Now there are a few night races on the F1 schedule, and the illuminated circuits are spectacles to behold. During the 2023 season, the following Grands Prix were held at night:

- The Bahrain Grand Prix in Sakhir, Bahrain
- The Saudi Arabian Grand Prix in Jeddah, Saudi Arabia
- The Singapore Grand Prix in Marina Bay, Singapore
- The Las Vegas Grand Prix in Las Vegas, Nevada

Q: What Grand Prix has had to have a safety car deployed every year since 2008?

A: The Formula 1 Singapore Grand Prix in Marina Bay began in 2008 (prior Singapore Grands Prix were for other race categories and had taken place at a different location). In every

single Formula 1 Singapore Grand Prix from 2008 to the time of this writing, a safety has had to be deployed either due to a stalled car or a crash.

Q: What are the rules for what tires are used on a race weekend?

A: Pirelli (the current sole supplier until at least the end of 2024) created eight types of 18-inch tires for the 2023 season: six slick varieties from C0 to C5, one intermediate variety, and one wet variety (see Chapter 4 for more details). But not all of the slick tires can be used on a race weekend. Three of them are picked by Pirelli based on the characteristics of the circuit and the area's climate, and the driver must use two of them during a race, except for Sprint races or if wet weather is forcing them to use wet or intermediate tires instead of the softer compounds, which means during dry-weather full Sunday races, the drivers each have to pit at least once.

The three dry-weather tires chosen for the weekend are given the following color coding: white for the hardest, yellow for the medium, and red for the softest. The intermediates are coded green and the wets blue. Each driver is supplied with three sets of wets, four sets of intermediates, and 13 sets of slicks on most weekends.

Q: What does it mean when someone says "box" or "box, box" over the radio in F1?

A: "Box, box" or "box" means the driver needs to return to the pit. It is often said over the radio by the driver's race engineer when a car has taken damage and is in need of repair. It comes from boxenstop, the German word for pit stop.

Q: What does it mean to retire during a race?

A: If things have gone wrong with a car during a race and it is either having too many mechanical problems or has taken too much damage, sometimes the team will make the call to retire the car, meaning the driver leaves the race permanently rather than pitting for repair.

Q: What might the race engineer say to the driver when they want them to speed up?

A: An engineer will tell a driver to push, or say "Push, push" when they want them to go full bore.

CHAPTER 6

PICKING UP SPEED

THE SCIENCE OF F1

Q: What is g-force?

A: G-force (aka acceleration force) is a force exerted on an object as it accelerates, decelerates, or changes direction. One g is one times the gravitational pull of the earth, which is 9.81 meters per second squared. Two g's would be two times that amount of force, three would be three times, and so on.

Q: How much g-force are drivers subjected to during an F1 race?

A: It all depends on what happens during the race, but modern F1 cars can exert four to five g's of force on drivers around corners and up to 6.5 when they brake. For comparison, regular car drivers typically experience less than one g, while fighter jet pilots can be subjected to up to 9 g's of force. One case in F1 (or any other vehicular activity) when g-forces exceed the norm is during a crash, when they can reach astronomical heights (see Chapter 12 for an example).

Q: What are the overcut and undercut strategies?

A: Both involve pitting for tire replacement to gain time on their competitors. The overcut involves pitting for fresh tires later in the race and using the extra grip to overtake the cars that pitted earlier. The undercut involves pitting for fresh tires earlier in the race and using the extra speed to overtake the cars that stayed out longer.

Q: What are oversteer and understeer in racing?

A: Both oversteer and understeer have to do with car steering responsiveness. Oversteer is when the car turns more than the driver expects, which can cause the rear of the car to lose grip

and slide into a skid. Understeer is the opposite, when the car turns less than the driver expects, which can cause the front of the car to lose grip and slide away from the apex on a turn.

Q: What is a slipstream in race driving?

A: A slipstream is an effect that occurs behind a race car on a straightaway where the area just behind the car has reduced air resistance. Another race car can follow closely behind to take advantage and gain speed due to decreased drag with the ultimate goal of slingshotting around and taking the lead. Around corners, however, this change in air resistance creates an effect called "dirty air" that can actually slow down a car following closely behind. A driver using the slipstream effect is sometimes called "distant tow" or "getting a tow."

Q: What is opposite-locking in racing?

A: Opposite-locking is when the car's rear wheels lose grip and the driver has to turn in the opposite direction from the direction they are trying to turn (think of the advice to turn into a skid).

Q: What physical change does an F1 driver typically go through over the course of one race?

A: F1 drivers typically lose six to eight pounds over the course of one race. This is mainly due to the cockpits of the cars heating up during racing to as high as 122°F, causing the driver to sweat a lot. In fact, drivers tend to lose more weight in humid climates. Drivers have to drink water on the course to prevent dehydration. And once the race is over, they are required to step on a scale and have their weight checked. But the weigh-in has a dual purpose: to make sure the driver hasn't lost too much weight and is in need of medical attention, and to make sure the car and driver are still above the F1 minimum weight requirement.

Q: What nifty trick can a driver use at the end of a race to increase their official weight?

A: Drivers will sometimes run over the marbles (small bits of tire rubber) that have accumulated past the finish line in the hopes of picking some up to increase weight, which is measured at the end of the race to make sure the car and driver aren't under the weight minimum.

Q: What advance in car design was introduced in 1977 and banned from 1982 to 2021?

A: The Lotus 78, driven by the team during the 1977 season, had a major speed advantage. The design was the introduction of ground-effect to Formula 1 cars, an innovation which was ultimately banned from 1982 to 2021 and allowed again starting in 2022. The ground-effect design involved changing the placement of the side pods and radiators and adding a skirt that brushed the ground. This airflow along with the skirts created a negative pressure under the car that sucked the car downward, so now it wasn't just the wings providing the downforce effect. Ground-effect designs also reduce the turbulent air the cars would produce behind them, which would affect drivers following close behind.

Q: At what speed does downforce come into play?

A: The extremely aerodynamic design of F1 and other race cars doesn't do a whole heck of a lot of good at speeds below 50 miles per hour. It is above this speed that the advantages of a car's aerodynamic design, like downforce, start to provide noticeable benefits.

Q: What law of fluid dynamics is used to aerodynamically design F1 cars to increase downforce?

A: The Bernoulli principle is a phenomenon described in fluid dynamics where the faster a fluid is moving, the lower the pressure, and the slower it's moving, the higher the pressure. The principle was discovered by Daniel Bernoulli and explained in his 1738 book Hydrodynamics. Air is a gas and gases (along with liquids) are fluids, making this principle useful in aerodynamics. Aerodynamic designs are used to make F1 cars go at fast speeds in relative safety. The shape of the cars' wings, which are curved downward at the top, makes the pressure higher above them and lower below them, resulting in downforce pushing the car down onto the track.

Q: What specific example of the Bernoulli principle is at play in tunnels underneath F1 cars utilizing ground-effects?

A: The Venturi effect is an application of the Bernoulli principle published by Giovanni Battista Venturi in 1797 that states that when a fluid flows through an area that goes from wider to more restrictive, the velocity of the fluid increases and the pressure decreases. Since the beginning of the 2022 season, F1 cars have been allowed to use ground-effects again and include Venturi tunnels underneath the car that cause the air to flow through areas that become constricted, decreasing air pressure and increasing the downforce that presses the car to the track.

Q: What did bargeboards on F1 cars do?

A: Starting with the McLaren MP4/8 during the 1993 Formula 1 season, many cars included bargeboards.

These were pieces that were attached on either side of a car between the front wheels and the sidelines to control airflow. But the changes in technical specifications starting in the 2022 F1 season that allowed ground-effects made bargeboards obsolete.

Q: What team's drivers were disqualified due to the bargeboards on their car?

A: During the 1999 Malaysian Grand Prix, Ferrari drivers Eddie Irvine and Michael Schumacher came in first and second place. But both were disqualified when scrutineers after the race decided that the F399 car's bargeboard broke regulations for being one centimeter too wide. The decision was appealed, and the FIA overturned it shortly afterward, stating that the measuring equipment of the FIA scrutineers at the Malaysia Grand Prix were not accurate enough to make that call. The drivers' disqualifications were overturned, and their wins were reinstated.

Q: What are wind tunnels and how are they used in F1?

A: Wind tunnels are testing equipment developed for the aeronautics industry but also useful for testing the aerodynamics of cars, especially fast cars like those driven in Formula 1. It is a tunnel with a huge powerful fan at one end that blows air at a high speed toward a stationary car or model of a car to simulate the airflow over a car moving at high speed through the air. Although stationary air with an object moving through it doesn't behave exactly the same as air being blown over a stationary object, wind tunnel tearing can still be used to gather data on such things as drag and downforce. These days the models are covered in sensors to gather as much data as possible. The Formula 1 rules were changed so that full-size cars and models couldn't be used in wind tunnel testing. Now they must be no more than 60 percent of the size of a real F1 car. And they can't run them at the full speed of an F1 car but are limited to around 110 miles per hour. The amount of time that an F1 car (or model) can be tested with a wind tunnel is limited, and to try to even out the performance of the cars, teams with lower points are allowed more time testing in the wind tunnel than teams with more points.

Q: Why do drivers weave back and forth during slow laps?

A: When driving during the out-lap during qualifying or practice, a formation lap, a lap taken behind a safety car, or a lap while the virtual safety car is activated, the drivers can often be seen weaving back and forth to the left and right, driving in a sort of sine-wave pattern rather than in a normal fashion. They do this to warm up the tires to improve their grip on the track and also to warm up the brakes. The constant swiveling means they are driving over a longer distance than if they just kept driving normally even though they are going slower.

Q: What is porpoising?

A: Most people like porpoises, but F1 drivers and teams are not fond of porpoising. A car is porpoising when the wheels stay on the ground but the rest of the car bounces up and down on its suspension. It is a potential side effect of the ground-effect aerodynamic designs that were reintroduced in the 2022 season, which increases downforce and effectively sucks the car down onto the track. Porpoising usually happens on the straightaways and is caused when the car gets too close to the ground, which blocks the airflow and negates the ground-effect downforce. The car rises, making the airflow resume, which increases downforce again and pushes the car back down, in a cycle that causes the bouncing. This phenomenon can affect a driver's performance as well as their comfort. The FIA introduced new technical specs for 2023 that raised the edge of the floor heights by 15 millimeters (about half an inch) to reduce the chance of porpoising, and it seems to have done the trick.

Q: What is flow-viz paint?

A: Flow-viz paint (or flow-vis), which stands for "flow visualization," is a concoction containing a fluorescent powder mixed with paraffin or another light oily substance used to see how the air is flowing around the vehicle. Flow-viz can be painted onto a model or an actual F1 car before testing in a wind tunnel or a practice run around a real track. As the car goes at those fast F1 speeds (or the wind tunnel simulates similar conditions), the oily mixture moves along the car, the oil evaporates and the paint dries, leaving tell-tale trails of fluorescent material that give loads of information about airflow to the aerodynamicists and designers.

SHIFTING GEARS

EVOLUTION OF THE SPORT

ⓠ Where and when was the FIA founded?

Ⓐ The Fédération Internationale de l'Automobile (FIA), the governing body of F1 and many other motorsports, was founded in Paris, France, as the Association Internationale des Automobile Clubs Reconnus (AIACR) in 1904, 46 years before Formula 1 was established as an official motorsport.

ⓠ Why was the organization that became the FIA formed?

Ⓐ In the early-twentieth century, motorsport was becoming popular, but there was no governing body, which made it unsafe and unfair. The organization then known as the Association Internationale des Automobile Clubs Reconnus was formed as a coalition of 13 separate motor clubs from multiple countries who sought to standardize motorsport rules and provide safety regulations. The effort was spearheaded by the Automobile Club de France (ACF).

ⓠ After what major world event was the AIACR renamed the FIA?

Ⓐ In the late 1930s and the first half of the 1940s, World War II raged across Europe, Asia, and numerous other parts of the globe. The motorsports overseen by the AIACR all went on hiatus during this time for obvious reasons (including safety and resources). In fact, many industries, including automotive industries, were conscripted to provide resources to the war effort (see Chapter 2's entry that mentions the Ascari Fiat dealership). The motorsports overseen by the AIACR resumed in 1946, the year after the war ended, and the organization changed its name to the FIA.

Q: Where are the headquarters of the FIA?

A: As of this writing, headquarters of the FIA are in both Paris, France, and Geneva, Switzerland.

Q: For what role has the EU deemed the FIA the sole oversight entity?

A: Under the laws of Europe, the FIA is in charge of assessing and certifying the safety of motorsport circuits and racing vehicles.

Q: How many motor and motorsport entities does the FIA represent?

A: As of 2023, the FIA has 241 motor- and motorsport-related clubs all over the world under its regulatory wing.

Q: How different were the cars at a given race in the early days of F1 compared to now?

A: The cars themselves driven during a given race used to be quite different from each other, back when the rulebook was only about a page long. As the FIA sporting and technical rules have become more complex, with design specifications spelled out down to millimeters of length and height and other metrics, the designs of the cars have become more homogeneous. This homogenization shifted into high gear when breakthroughs in aerodynamics began to be applied to Formula 1 cars.

🅠 Have the rules regarding team and driver numbers always been as strict as they are today?

🅐 Just like the rules for the cars, the rules for the team configurations and numbers of participants were loosey-goosey in the early days of the sport. Most of the rules in the 1950s had to do with the engines of the cars. Teams could have one or more drivers, not two like today. Cars could be swapped to other drivers during races, and teams didn't have to participate in every Grand Prix event.

🅠 What changes have the F1 regulations undergone over the decades?

🅐 The regulations in Formula 1 have changed vastly over the decades. In 1950, the F1 regulations fit on three pages, with the technical regulations fitting on only one and consisting of just a few simple specifications. The cars had to be four-wheeled, have either a 1.5-liter supercharged engine or a 4.5-liter naturally aspirated engine, have fire protection between the engine and the driver, and have two rear-view mirrors for keeping an eye on passing cars. These days, the FIA creates three separate rule-books every year: technical, sporting, and financial regulations. In 2023, all three together equaled over 300 pages.

🅠 What power unit component is being removed starting in 2026?

🅐 The FIA has decided that starting in 2026, the innovative but complex and expensive MGU-H will no longer be part of the F1 car specifications (see Chapter 4 for more detail on the MGU-H and its counterpart, the MGU-K). This is in part to decrease the cost of producing an F1 engine and to hopefully allow more manufacturers to participate.

Q: What is a major reason for many of the regulations?

A: Improving the safety of the sport, often by keeping the cars from becoming too fast, has been behind many of the rule changes. The faster the car, the higher the chance of injury or death (to drivers, other F1 personnel, and spectators alike) in the case of an accident on the track. And recently, there have also been rule changes to reduce emissions and make the cars more eco-friendly.

Q: Why was refueling banned in 2010?

A: F1 racers used to be able to refuel during a pit stop, but the practice was banned in 2010 for safety reasons. Two notable previous incidents included one in 1994 at the German Grand Prix in Hockenheim when Benetton driver Jos Verstappen's vehicle was sprayed with gasoline and then set alight, and another in 2009 at the Brazilian Grand Prix when a fuel hose didn't detach from driver Heiiki Kovalainen's vehicle, got dragged, and set driver Kimi Raikkonen on fire! Thank goodness for fire-resistant suits.

Q: What had to be increased as a result of the 2010 refueling ban?

A: The minimum weight allowance for F1 cars had to be increased by the FIA to allow them to accommodate the larger gas tanks and extra fuel needed to race without refueling. 2023 F1 cars hold about 110 kg (around 29 gallons) of fuel, and it has to be enough to last the entire race.

Q: What is the weight requirement for a Formula 1 car?

A: This figure changes from year to year. In 2023, the minimum weight of an F1 car was 798 kilograms (around 1,759 pounds) without fuel, but including tires, the driver, and their gear. There is no maximum weight, but teams try to keep the weight low to ensure that they are competitively fast.

Q: What is the F1 Academy?

A: The F1 Academy is a new racing series that began in 2023. Its aim is to encourage and develop young female drivers to participate in the Formula 1 pipeline. Each team has three drivers. To make it more affordable, F1 Academy provides a subsidy for 150,000 euros per vehicle (around 162,000 US dollars) to be matched by the driver. The teams and drivers in the inaugural season are:

- ➲ ART Grand Prix: Lena Buhler, Carrie Schreiner, and Chloe Grant
- ➲ Campos Racing: Nerea Marti, Lola Lovinfosse, and Maite Carceres
- ➲ MP Motorsport: Hamda Al Qubaisi, Emely de Heus, and Amna Al Qubaisi
- ➲ PREMA Racing: Chloe Chong, Marta Garcia, and Bianca Bustamante
- ➲ Rodin Carlin: Abbi Pulling, Jessica Edgar, and Megan Gilkes

Q: What was the only all-female single-seater championship before F1 Academy?

A: The W Series was an all-female single-seater racing series that lasted from 2019 to 2022.

SHOW ME THE MONEY

EXPENSES, SPONSORSHIPS, AND WINNINGS

Q: How much does it take to run a Formula 1 team for a season?

A: The answer is loads! Running Formula 1 is incredibly expensive. It takes a lot of cutting-edge equipment, a dedicated staff of everyone from car engineers to pit crew to chefs, and of course top-notch drivers. Running a Formula 1 team takes tens to hundreds of millions of dollars. To keep things a little fairer for the less wealthy teams, in 2021 the FIA instituted a budget limit of $145 million per team, set to go down by $5 million per year. This amount excludes marketing, engine development, and driver salaries. Some teams' budgets had ballooned to around $300 million before the rule change.

Q: Is Formula 1 the most expensive sport?

A: Formula 1 is terribly expensive and is often cited as the most expensive sport, at least in recent years, even after the budget cap (see above). Other runners up are other motorsports, as well as things like equestrian sports and polo (where maintaining horses costs a pretty penny) and yacht racing. See Chapter 11 for a sporting event that gave Formula 1 a run for its money (budget-wise) in 2009 and 2010.

Q: How much can an F1 driver make?

A: Drivers' salaries vary and have definitely gone up over the years. In 2023, a full-time driver's pay ranged from $1 million to $65 million. Their pay comes in the form of a base salary plus bonuses for performance. But they can also make money via winnings, endorsements, and sponsorships. The top earner, likely because he's won the last three World Championships, is Red Bull Racing driver Max Verstappen. Mercedes driver Lewis

Hamilton is the next highest paid, followed by Ferrari driver Charles LeClerc.

Q: Do drivers have to pay fees to the FIA?

A: The answer is yes. They have to pay annually for their Super Licence (see Chapter 3 for more details). And at a base fee reported to be over $12,000 plus an additional fee for each point scored in the previous World Championship, it can really add up, especially for the winners. Max Verstappen reportedly had to pay over $1 million to race in the 2023 season.

Q: What is the Concorde Agreement?

A: The Concorde Agreement is a commercial contract that was originally written up and adopted in 1981 at a time of turmoil in the sport when there was infighting between FISA (later the FIA) and F1 teams. The agreement has since been the law of the land and spells out the rights and roles of the three major stakeholders in Formula 1: the FIA, the commercial entity known as Formula 1, and the F1 teams.

Q: How are rule-change decisions made according to the Concorde Agreement?

A: Prior to 2021, rule changes had to be unanimously agreed to by the FIA, Formula 1, and the teams. Since a 2021 change, it now only takes eight teams plus Formula 1 and the FIA to agree to a rule change, although Ferrari has veto power. Each group is assigned 10 votes. Twenty-five votes are required to make changes for the upcoming season. And 28 are required to make immediate changes.

Q: Why would a potential new F1 team be required to pay a fee of $200 million?

A: The commercial income generated by Formula 1 is doled out between the 10 existing teams (at the time of this writing). The $200 million would help make up for the fact that a new team would be taking a new share of the commercial income.

Q: How much is the total prize money doled out to the winners in modern Formula 1?

A: Per the Concorde Agreement, the prize money is 50 percent of Formula 1's commercial profit, with some stipulations for a larger percentage to F1 management after a certain amount of revenue. In 2022, the prize money equaled around $1.157 billion. It is expected to be even higher in 2023.

Q: What is the stock ticker symbol for Formula 1 Group?

A: The ticker symbol used by NASDAQ to designate Formula 1 Group (Liberty Media Corp) stock is FWON.

Q: What was the first F1 team to emblazon their cars with a sponsor's colors?

A: At the nonchampionship 1967 Rhodesian Grand Prix in Bulawayo, new privateer Team Gunston's Brabham BT20 cars featured the colors of Gunston, a South African cigarette company. One of their drivers, John Love, even came in first. They didn't fare as well at the championship South African Grand Prix in 1968, but their cars still sported the company colors and name. Lotus followed suit when team boss Colin Chapman sent letters to dozens of British companies seeking sponsorship, resulting in the team racing the non-F1 Tasman

Series that year with their cars painted in the Gold Leaf Tobacco colors along with the company logo, with the F1 cars following suit during the 1968 season. The rest is sponsorship history.

Q: What industry's branding was featured on every title-winning F1 car from 1984 to 2007?

A: Every car that won an F1 title from 1984 to 2007 featured the branding of a tobacco company. Cigarette ads were so ubiquitous in Formula 1 for decades that Marlboro ads even made it onto billboards in the 1982 video game Pole Position.

Q: When did tobacco sponsorship in F1 decrease drastically?

A: It almost seems as if tobacco advertising no longer exists in F1, but there is still a minor amount. In 2006, the FIA recommended (but did not mandate) that Formula 1 teams stop making sponsorship deals with tobacco companies. Since then, there has been little sponsorship from the tobacco industry. However, Ferrari still partnered with Phillip Morris until 2021. And McLaren still has a deal with British American Tobacco, but only for its lower-risk products (like vaping products and oral nicotine pouches).

Q: Who has the media rights to broadcast F1 competitions?

A: ESPN pays a hefty sum for the media rights to Formula 1 events. The most recent contract between Formula 1 and ESPN, signed in 2022, reportedly gives the network the rights through 2025 at an annual cost estimated to be somewhere over $75 million.

Q: What is a title sponsorship?

A: A title sponsorship is a sponsorship so lucrative that the sponsor gets their name on the title of the team. They are reported to cost as much as $70 million. The following are the full team names of the 2024 teams with title sponsors included in the name:

- Mercedes-AMG PETRONAS F1 Team—Petronas is an energy company.
- BWT Alpine F1 Team—BWT is a water treatment company in Austria.
- MoneyGram Haas F1 Team—MoneyGram is an international payment company.
- Oracle Red Bull Racing—Oracle is a software and cloud infrastructure company.
- Aston Martin Aramco F1—Aramco is an energy and chemical company.
- Visa Cash App RB Formula 1 Team—RB has two title sponsors: Visa is a major credit card company and Cash App is a mobile payment company.
- Stake F1 Team Kick Sauber—Stake is an online casino and sports betting company.

The McLaren, Ferrari, and Williams teams do not have title sponsorships.

Q: Approximately how much do sponsor logos on the cars cost?

A: A bunch of places on F1 cars are decked out with sponsor logos and ads, ranging from small individual logos to the whole car decked out in the main sponsor's branding and colors. Company branding can be placed on the front and rear wings, the nose, the side pods, the mirrors, and the halo (anywhere that's outwardly visible to the crowd, really). Small logos start at $1 million, medium in the $5 million range, and large around $25 million. Title sponsor branding and colors all over the car is currently around $70 million!

Q: What other places do sponsor logos and ads appear in F1?

A: Sponsorship advertising doesn't just appear on cars. There are also track-side banners and billboards throughout the circuit. And the drivers themselves wear logos all over their race suits and helmets, and even on the non-racing outfits they wear at races and promotional events. When they take off their helmets after a race, they are often handed a branded cap to wear. And the full names of many of the teams include their title sponsor names, which is advertising in and of itself. Even Grands Prix bear sponsor names these days, like the Lenovo Chinese Grand Prix and the Rolex Belgian Grand Prix.

Q: Can individual drivers get sponsorships?

A: Not all sponsorships are made directly with the teams. The drivers can also make sponsorship deals and feature sponsor logos on their car or their personal gear and clothing. They can also sponsor products and appear in advertising.

CHAPTER 9

BACKSEAT DRIVERS

NON-DRIVER JOBS IN F1

Q: How big are the staffs of modern Formula 1 teams?

A: Drivers are key to the success of Formula 1, but it takes multitudes to run Formula 1 competitions and teams. The teams themselves each employ a great many people behind the scenes. Among the current teams, some have over 800 employees in roles spanning from commercial to sporting to technical areas of racing. Around 100 of them travel with the team to Grand Prix race weekends. As of this writing, the number of staff a team is allowed to bring to the track on race weekends is 115, and only 58 are allowed to work directly on the cars.

Q: What is the head of an F1 team called?

A: At the head of it all is the team principal, aka the team boss, who oversees the entire team. Their duties include acquiring funding, recruiting drivers and other top people to run the various departments, and basically calling all the shots with the aim of driving the team to win races and championships.

Q: Who are the current F1 team principals?

A: There has been a lot of turnover of team bosses in the last couple of years. Two are just starting at the beginning of the 2024 season. These are the team bosses of the current 10 Formula 1 teams as of January 2024:

- Alessandro Alunni Bravi—Stake Sauber. Started 2023.
- Bruno Famin—Alpine. Started 2023.
- Christian Horner—Red Bull Racing. Started 2005.
- Ayao Komatsu—Haas. Started 2024.
- Mike Krack—Aston Martin. Started 2022.

⮑ Laurent Mekies—AlphaTauri RB. Started 2024.

⮑ Andrea Stella—McLaren. Started 2022.

⮑ Fred Vasseur—Ferrari. Started 2022.

⮑ James Vowles—Williams. Started 2023.

⮑ Toto Wolff—Mercedes. Started 2013.

Q: What is a race engineer?

A: Each driver has their own race engineer. This person works closely with the driver to help them get the most out of the vehicle. The engineer might examine a racetrack and get feedback from the driver to tweak the setup parameters of the car for a given race. They also take their driver's driving style into account.

Q: Who sits on the pit wall?

A: Each team has a portion of their crew up on the pit wall during a race, usually top people like the team boss and heads of the various departments, in a pit stand that the team sets up itself. But the pit wall setup and crew is different for every team. They wear headsets so that they can communicate with others on their crew at the race, and even with team members back at the factory. They have displays that allow them to see a great deal, including the race itself via the regular race feed, their drivers' cars via the car cameras, telemetry information from the cars themselves, GPS information on the cars' locations, lap times, and information about the weather, among other things. At Monaco there is no literal pit wall and the pit stand is on top of the garage.

@? What is a pit board?

A? Pit boards are physical boards that teams can hang over the pit wall to communicate information to their drivers, like how many laps there are to go or any instructions the team wants the driver to follow. They have large replaceable letters and numbers and don't contain too much information so as not to confuse the drivers.

@? Who has been the Formula 1 safety car driver since 2000?

A? The F1 safety car isn't just a general term, nor is safety car driver. As of this writing, one driver has been on the job since the year 2000! That driver is Bernd Mayländer, a former DTM and FIA GT series driver from Germany. And the current safety car is a Mercedes AMG GT R.

@? What are the different jobs within a pit crew?

A? The pit crew does not mess around when a driver zooms (at the proper speed limit) into the pit. Pit stops often last as little as two-and-a-half seconds! Part of the way they achieve this incredible speed and efficiency is through a very organized pit crew structure, where each member has a certain job they need to perform flawlessly and in sync with everyone else. A typical pit crew might include:

- Two jack operators who respectively lift the front and back of the car, with two more backup jack operators just in case.

- Twelve tire personnel—three for each tire—consisting of one person to loosen and tighten the lug nuts, one to remove the old tire, and one to put on the new tire.

➲ Two people on either side of the car to stabilize it while it's up on the jacks. They may also play double duty by cleaning the driver's visor, the mirrors, or other parts of the car.

➲ One person on each corner of the front wing to make adjustments.

➲ One person to control the traffic lights, formerly a "lollipop man" (see Chapter 1), to signal the driver to stay put, when to put the car in first gear, and when to take off back onto the track, with an additional person watching for issues from the side who can keep the driver from being signaled to take off if needed.

Other mechanics might come into play if the car needs repairs or part replacements. But the above crew members are necessary for a typical pit stop. Many practice pit stops are performed every race weekend to make sure the crew is on point at race time.

@? What safety equipment and measures do the pit crew have to use?

△? Just like drivers, the pit crew is required to wear fire-resistant Nomex suits, helmets, and eye protection. The crew are only allowed out of their garage and into the pit area just before one of their team's cars gets to the pit stop. The crew must make sure the car is in safe driving condition and that the pit lane is clear of other cars before they release their driver back into the race. To protect the pit crew, the driver must drive at or below the 80 kilometer (a little under 50 miles) per hour speed limit in the pit lane and they are also not allowed to reverse the car in the pit lane. If the car must be moved backward in this area, the pit crew has to push it that way.

Q: What's a dummy stop?

A: Formula 1 is competitive on many levels: driver against all other drivers (including teammates) and team against all other teams. Sometimes things are done to try to psych out the others and get an advantage. One of these things is a dummy stop, where the pit crew runs toward the pit to make other teams think they are pitting one of their drivers in the hopes that it will make another team bring their own driver in too soon.

Q: What is a wheel gun?

A: A wheel gun is the tool some of the pit crew in charge of changing the tires use to remove and then tighten the lug nuts on the wheels so that the tires can be replaced. The tool does its job in a flash and is part of the reason pit stops are so short these days.

Q: Who lays out the design of circuits?

A: Circuits are complicated, and special racetrack designers, or architects, are enlisted to create new circuits or modify existing ones. Some notable current racetrack architects are Hermann Tilke and Vanessa Mientus.

Q: What former Formula 1 driver and brother of multiple World Champion wins now provides commentary for Formula 1 races?

A: Ralf Schumacher, younger brother of seven-time World Champion Michael Schumacher, is a commentator for Sky News. See Chapter 3 for more on his Formula 1 career.

Q: Which commentator was in a famous accident at the Australia Grand Prix?

A: At the very first F1 Australia Grand Prix that was held at Melbourne in 1996, Martin Brundle (who went from racing to commentating) hit and drove up Johnny Herbert's Sauber vehicle, launching Brundle's car into the air, where it did a somersault over both Herbert's and David Coulthard's cars and then flew off the track. Amazingly, he hopped out of his car and ran to get approval to resume racing in the team's spare car. He ended up wrecking again, but far less seriously, but that retired him from the race.

Q: What volunteer position is integral to the safety of F1 races?

A: Marshals are the people who wave flags to alert drivers of track conditions and run onto the track when there is an accident, sometimes putting out fires or providing first aid. They are absolutely vital to the safety and smooth running of a Formula 1 race. And amazingly, they are all unpaid volunteers!

Q: What division of the FIA handles driver and team contract disputes?

A: Contractual disputes within teams are handled by the Contract Recognition Board (CRB).

Q: What does a scrutineer do in Formula 1?

A: A scrutineer inspects the cars to make sure they comply with all the rules for Formula 1 racing.

Q: What is the Formula One Group?

A: The Formula One Group began as the Formula One Constructors' Association (FOCA) in 1974. It is a collection of companies that control the commercial rights and promotion of Formula 1 as recognized by the Concorde Agreement.

Q: What company bought the Formula One Group in 2017?

A: The Formula One Group was acquired by Liberty Media Corporation in early 2017, after which they renamed their company the Formula One Group. Existing Chairman Chase Carey was made chief executive officer, and Bernie Ecclestone was made chairman emeritus.

Q: Who is the current president of the FIA?

A: As of this writing, the president of the FIA is Mohammed Ben Sulayem from the United Arab Emirates. He was voted into the FIA presidency in 2021. A former rally racer, Sulayem's racing career spanned from 1983 to 2002, during which he won the title of Middle East Rally Champion 14 times.

Q: How often is the presidency of the FIA up for election?

A: The FIA holds an election to choose the new president of the FIA every four years.

Q: Who is CEO of Formula 1?

A: The Formula 1 organization is a separate entity from the FIA and the individual teams (see Chapter 7 for more on their role in the sport). As of this writing, its CEO is Stefano Domenicali. He is a former longtime Ferrari employee and team boss, with stints as AUDI AG as a vice president and Automobili Lamborghini as CEO. He also served as president of the FIA Single Seater Commission.

Q: Why are team chefs so important?

A: A race car runs on fuel, but so do their drivers! F1 teams have their own chefs who prepare food for the drivers, the team's staff, and even guests, including VIPs and press. Feeding the drivers is their most important task as the drivers need to eat at certain times and have stricter nutritional requirements than others. But the pit crew and other team members need to keep their energy up, as well. F1 chefs start early and end late on race days, often working very long hours. Some teams even have chefs with Michelin stars!

RUBBERNECKING

SPECTATING F1

Q: What sort of seats can you get to watch a Formula 1 race?

A: All circuits and Grands Prix have differences, but at a typical circuit, you can buy one of three types of tickets to the race:

- ➲ General admission—These tickets are usually for standing-room-only areas along the outskirts of the racetrack.

- ➲ Center pass—These tickets are also standing-room but allow you to spectate from the center of the track.

- ➲ Grandstand—These tickets get you a reserved seat in a grandstand, which tend to be situated in good spots to get a glimpse of the teams and the action.

Q: How much do tickets to F1 Grands Prix cost?

A: The ticket price for Formula 1 races run the gamut and depend greatly on the circuit and the location of the seats. They can range from less than $100 to thousands of dollars.

Q: How can you watch F1 at home?

A: Currently in the United States, live Formula 1 races are broadcast on certain ESPN channels, which you can access via some cable or streaming services. You can also subscribe to F1 TV to view live races, or pay more for their F1 TV Pro service to also watch older races on demand.

Q: What allows you to participate in your own incorporeal Formula 1 season?

A: Baseball and football don't have a monopoly on fantasy leagues. You can also enter your own teams in the official

Formula 1 Fantasy competition. Players can even win prizes, from gift cards to the F1 store all the way up to tickets to a Grand Prix.

Q: What is a sponsor day?

A: Teams and their sponsors will sometimes have sponsor promotional days on non-race days, when fans can come for various festivities and sometimes even meet the drivers!

Q: Can a fan visit an F1 team's factory?

A: Yes, on certain occasions. Some of the teams open their factories to visitors on specific days.

Q: How can a fan show their allegiance to a team or driver?

A: Fans can of course buy their team's branded shirts and other merchandise in the team colors. And they can (and often do) wave flags to show the team and drivers who they are rooting for.

Q: Can a regular person drive an F1 car?

A: Most people aren't allowed to drive the newer Formula 1 cars, unless they're someone like Tom Cruise (see Chapter 14). But there are outfits that allow regular people to pay for F1 driving experiences, usually in 20-or-so-year-old Formula 1 cars that were actually driven in races. They aren't quite as fast and high-tech as the latest and greatest, but they can certainly give one the feel of driving F1. The cost is usually a few thousand and includes training and practice laps in non-F1 vehicles before putting the participant in the Formula 1 vehicle for a few laps around the track. Some even allow you to drive on actual F1 circuits!

Q: Are there any multi-seat Formula 1 vehicles?

A: Surprisingly, the answer is yes! Sort of. Although they weren't ever actually used in Formula 1 races in their multi-seat form, some manufacturers have made two-seater and three-seater Formula 1 cars so that a driver could take passengers on the ride of their lives. The earliest two-seater was McLaren's 1998 MP4-98T (the T standing for two) created for promotional purposes. The first three-seater was from Arrows team in 2001, whose owner Tom Walkinshaw had the Arrows AX3 three-seater built from cannibalized Arrow A21 Formula 1 cars driven by Jos Verstappen and Pedro de la Rosa in the previous Formula 1 season. Other three- and two-seaters have since been built by other F1 manufacturers for training, promotion, VIP rides, and even F1 experiences for fans.

CHAPTER 11

OFF THE BEATEN PATH
RELATED MOTORSPORTS

Q: What is a feeder sport?

A: A feeder sport in F1 is another single-seater open-wheeled motorsport that feeds talent into F1. IndyCar can be considered a feeder sport into Formula 1, but the more official route is F4 to F Regional, to F3, to F2, to F1. These are all considered training grounds for future F1 racers. Read on to find out more about these feeder series as well as other similar current non-F1 series.

Q: What are the main FIA "Formula" racing series besides Formula 1?

A: Since 2014, the FIA recognizes four main tiers below the Formula 1 series. All use open-wheeled single-seater vehicles similar to F1 cars, but not quite as advanced, powerful, or expensive as the F1 cars, which have 1,000 or so horsepower 1.6-liter V6 turbocharged power units and other cutting-edge tech. The following are the main Formula series below F1:

➲ Formula 2 (formerly GP2) is the tier just below Formula 1 in the racing hierarchy that feeds into F1. In F2, at the time of this writing, the rules stipulate using cars with a turbocharged 3.4-liter V6 engine that generates around 620 horsepower. Unlike F1, all F2 cars have the same engine and chassis. They also don't have the extra hybrid components of F1, but they do now have DRS as of 2015. F2 races take place at the same locations and weekends as F1 races, but not all F1 weekends. There were only 11 F2 weekends in the 2023 season. The format is also a little different with only one practice round, one qualifying round, two short sprint races (where the starting positions of the top 10 drivers are actually the reverse of where they come in during qualifying), and a feature race (where the starting positions are in order of qualifying).

⮑ Formula 3 is the next tier below Formula 2 (formerly separate GP3 and Formula 3 European Championship series, which have now both been merged into a single Formula 3 series). At the time of this writing, its rules stipulate that the cars have a 3.4-liter naturally aspirated (rather than turbocharged) V6 engine of approximately 380 horsepower. In fact, they use the same engines as F2 cars. They are also lacking in the hybrid power unit technologies of F1 cars, but as of 2017, do have DRS. Since 2019, F3 Grands Prix have taken place at the same locations and weekends as Formula 1 races, with 10 scheduled for the 2023 season (although one at Imola, Italy, in May had to be canceled). The practice, qualifying, and races are much the same as F2, except that in the sprint races, the top 12 qualifying drivers start in reverse order on the grid for the sprint races.

⮑ Formula Regional competitions are held by separate regional entities. As of this writing, the FIA-approved Formula Regional championships include the European Championship, Americas Championship, Asian Championship, Japanese Championship, Indian Championship, Oceania Championship, and Middle East Championship. The car specs vary by region, but they hover close to the 2019 F3 specs when the cars used 1.8-liter engines.

⮑ Formula 4, having been introduced in 2014, is a new series created by the FIA as a relatively affordable bridge between karting and the Formula series for young up-and-coming drivers. The races and championships are regional rather than global. Unlike F2 and F3, there are four chassis suppliers and six engine suppliers for the teams to choose from. The engines are all 160-horsepower 4-cylinder engines, but they can be turbocharged (or not) and the engines currently range between 1.4 and 2.0 liter. The practice, qualifying, and race formats vary by region.

Q: What is the all-electric FIA Formula series?

A: Formula E (Formula Electric) is the all-electric Formula series, which began in 2017. Just as F1 serves as a test bed for car companies' future road car technology, Formula E serves as a test bed for future electric car innovations. The newest FE car, the Gen3, introduced in the 2023 season, can reach up to (and possibly over) 200 miles per hour. The Gen3 engine is 469-horsepower (a pretty big jump up from Gen2's 335 horsepower). But it also has a second 335-horsepower engine attached to the front axle to reclaim energy from regenerative braking. To add to the sustainability, they even recycled parts of the Gen2 cars to make some of the Gen3 parts. They also use sustainably sourced tire and battery materials and recycle the tires and battery cells. Unlike all the other Formula series and other open-wheeled racing vehicles, the newest Formula E doesn't have rear brakes at all. The race weekend formats are very similar to F1 except the races only last around 45 minutes.

Q: What are some other Formula series?

A: There are lots of other series that start with the word Formula, some defunct and some still going. Some of these include Formula 1000, Formula 3000 (defunct), Formula 5000,

Formula Ford, Formula Palmer Audi, and Formula Renault, but there are many others.

Q: What is Formula Libre?

A: Formula Libre isn't exactly a racing series but is a name often given to open-wheeled, single-seater racing for which the sky is (almost) the limit as far as rules go. Formula Libre races see a lot of different types of cars compete against each other.

Q: Which Formula 1 driver's brother stepped up into Formula 2 in 2023?

A: French driver Arthur LeClerc, brother of Formula 1 Ferrari driver Charles LeClerc, was promoted from Formula 3 to Formula 2 for the 2023 season.

Q: What terrible accident befell Michael Schumacher?

A: Michael Schumacher is alive as of this writing, but in 2013, he was involved in a terrible skiing accident. Since that time, his family has kept quiet on his condition for reasons of privacy, but he is reportedly being taken care of by his wife Corinna.

Q: Is Le Mans part of Formula 1?

A: No, the 24 Hours of Le Mans competition is a 24-hour endurance race where the drivers drive sports cars, which are quite different from the open-wheeled, single-seater cars of the various Formula series, and a lot closer to normal street cars. Although F1 drivers have participated in Le Mans, they don't drive their F1 race cars, which are not built to withstand racing for that long.

Q: What other motorsport used to be part of the F1 World Championship but isn't any longer?

A: From 1950 to 1961, the Indianapolis 500 (Indy500 for short) in the United States was officially part of the Formula 1 World Championship, although the Indy500 is just one IndyCar race. Read on to find out more about this similar but different racing series.

Q: How does IndyCar differ from F1?

A: IndyCar is an American high-level open-wheeled single-seater competition much like F1, but there are lots of notable differences.

Technology

- IndyCar vehicles have 2.2-liter twin-turbo V6 engines, versus F1's 1.6-liter turbo V6 power units. They have lower horsepower than Formula 1 cars, at 600 to 750 horsepower compared to F1's 1,000 horsepower engines.

- IndyCar tanks hold about 10 gallons less fuel and races like the Indianapolis 500 are 200 laps of 2.5 miles each (500 miles total).

- IndyCars can go from 0 to 200 miles per hour in around eight seconds, while F1 cars can do so in about four.

- All IndyCar engines are currently supplied by one of two companies: Honda or Chevrolet. F1 cars have had hybrid features for a while, but IndyCar just now introduced hybrid powertrains in 2024.

- IndyCar engines use 85 percent ethanol fuel (E85) whereas F1 engines use 10 percent ethanol fuel (E10).

- All IndyCar vehicles use the same aerodynamic fixtures and chassis, making them more like each other than F1 cars are.

- IndyCars also cost a lot less, at around $10 million a car.

- Rather than a Halo, IndyCar vehicles have a partially enclosed safety screen called an "aeroscreen."

- There are different compounds for tires like in F1, but all are supplied by Firestone, and they are 15-inch rather than 18-inch.

- Rather than DRS, IndyCars have a push-to-pass system that boosts their engine power by about 50 horsepower that they can use around 200 seconds per race (at most competitions) with no limitation on when and where they can use it on the circuit.

Competion

- IndyCar races take place on oval, street or road circuits, whereas F1 is devoid of oval circuits. The number of teams and drivers isn't as fixed in IndyCar as they are in F1.

- There is no driving allowed on ovals in the rain, but there are wet tires for street circuits. In F1, driving in the rain is allowed on any circuit, but races can be canceled if the weather makes it too dangerous.

- Pit stops take longer (around 10 seconds) in IndyCar because aside from changing tires, they can (and often must) refuel.

- There were 17 IndyCar races versus 23 Formula 1 races in 2023.

- F1 competitions take place all over the world, whereas all but one IndyCar race have taken place in the United States (the one exception being a 2019 race in Toronto, Ontario, in Canada).

- Current teams have one to six drivers, and the number of overall drivers can change from race to race.

- The point systems are also different, with IndyCar generally awarding higher numbers of points to drivers.

- And rather than each team competing for points, it's the engine manufacturers (currently Honda and Chevy) who compete for points alongside the drivers every year.

Q: What are the most common categories of race car?

A: There are several different types of race car used in various types of race series. These include:

- Single-seater, open-wheeled vehicles are used in the various series that start with the word Formula (including Formula 1) and in the IndyCar series.

- Sports cars are much like, and sometimes actually are, the production models of car companies' high-performance sports cars. These often look the most like regular cars (and again, sometimes are high-performance road cars), although there are prototype series where the cars are a little more out there in design. One of the most famous sports car races is the 24 Hours of Le Mans.

- Production cars (or showroom stock) are unmodified or slightly modified vehicles from car manufacturers.

- Rally cars are also much like production cars but are often modified with four-wheel drive and other things to make them suited for off-road driving.

- Touring cars are a lot like regular street cars, although they are modified for racing. Touring car racing is more prevalent in Europe, Britain, and Australia than in the US.

- Stock cars used to be modified production cars, but now, although they resemble sporty street cars on the outside, they no longer have many stock parts and are not street legal. NASCAR is the most famous stock car series.

- Dragsters are often long, wedge-shaped specialized cars used in drag racing that deploy parachutes out the back to slow them down. But regular and slightly modified cars can also be used in drag racing, which is really just lining up side-by-side and racing in a straight line.

Q: What type of race cars can go faster than F1 cars?

A: IndyCars can reach up to 240 miles per hour compared to F1's 220 or so top speeds. And some dragsters can exceed 300 miles per hour! But only for a brief period and only in a straight line. In F1, IndyCar, and most other racing series, the drivers have to slow down to corner, so the average overall race speeds are lower than the top possible speed.

Q: Which are faster: Le Mans Hypercars or F1 race cars?

A: Although both can reach speeds over 200 miles per hour, Formula 1 race cars beat Le Mans Hypercars in overall lap speed. Le Mans rules allow for more powerful engines, but the Hypercars are heavier and less aerodynamic than F1 vehicles, which slows Hypercars down, especially around corners.

Q: How is an F1 circuit different from a NASCAR track?

A: Formula 1 circuits are road-racing tracks, whereas the ones used by NASCAR are oval tracks. Road tracks simulate the twists and turns and driving conditions on real roads (and in some cases like Monaco, Singapore, and Las Vegas, they are on real public roads blocked off for the competition). NASCAR is run on tracks that are (mostly) oval in shape and the turns are banked at various angles, meaning the outside of the track is higher in elevation than the inside track, making the cars drive at an angle. This banking brings centripetal force into the equation and allows the cars to take corners without flying off the track like they would if they cornered fast on a flat road track. Formula 1 cars are made for more typical roads and would not be safe on banked oval tracks. For one, they don't do well in side-on collisions with walls, which happens a lot more on oval tracks.

Q: What motorsports event has met or exceeded the cost of Formula 1?

A: In 2009 and 2010, an event called the Whitianga Festival of Speed was held in Whitianga, New Zealand. Cost-wise it was as expensive, if not more expensive, than Formula 1 racing due to the fact that it comprised multiple events using a lot of expensive vehicles, including helicopters, planes, power boats, various types of race cars, motorcycles, go-carts, parachutes, and jet skis. Some of the events were spectacles or displays of talent, like airshows and drifting and a demolition derby, while others were actual races. There were even cross-genre races, including helicopters versus powerboats and helicopters versus rally cars!

Q: What differentiates F1 cars from stock cars?

A: Formula 1 is not a stock car race because F1 teams build their cars from the ground up (even through many teams have to buy parts from engine and other part manufacturers). Originally, stock cars were regular cars that were in stock (thus the name) from regular car manufacturers, but that people used for racing. Some would be modified to have faster engines, better suspension, or other improvements, but they were largely just like regular cars. Today's stock cars for racing are not off-the-shelf models, so to speak, but heavily custom made for motorsports, maybe with a few stock parts. But they still resemble regular cars more than single-seater motorsport vehicles do.

Q: What famous variety of stock car racing owes some of its early history to Prohibition?

A: The 18th amendment of the US constitution, which made the production and sale of alcohol illegal in the country, was signed in 1919, went into effect in 1920, and was repealed in 1933. During this era, which we call the Prohibition Era, people were still drinking. They were just being supplied alcohol illegally. In the southeastern United States, many bootleggers had to quickly transport their illegal moonshine and other alcohols to buyers. This would often be done with souped-up Fords and other vehicles of the time, driven by fast drivers. Some of these drivers started racing each other on makeshift tracks. Eventually, this pastime evolved into a legitimate organized racing venture, starting in 1936 when the city of Daytona, Florida, hosted the first organized stock car race. Bill France, a race car driver and former mechanic for bootleggers, created the National Association for Stock Car Auto Racing (otherwise known as NASCAR). NASCAR held its first official race in 1948 in Daytona, and the winner was former moonshine runner Red Byron. Like Byron, many of the early drivers and mechanics got their starts working in the illegal alcohol running trade.

CHAPTER 12

INTERNATIONAL INCIDENTS
TRAGIC ACCIDENTS IN THE SPORT

Q: Who was the first F1 fatality?

A:)The Indy500 used to be part of the Formula 1 World Championship (see Chapter 11 for more details). And during this time, the F1 fatality rate was higher than that of other circuits. The first F1 fatality was Chet Miller at the 1953 Indianapolis 500 practice round, when he crashed into a concrete barrier after losing control of his car (a Novi Special).

Q: How did Carl Scarborough die at the 1953 Indy500?

A: Sadly, Chet Miller wasn't the only fatality at the 1953 Indy500 in Indianapolis (see above). Racecars get hot and overheat their drivers on the nicest of days, but during this race, it was so hot outside that three drum majorettes fainted, Pat Flaherty blacked out and hit a wall (but thankfully wasn't badly injured), and nine drivers had their cars taken over by relief drivers due to the heat. One of these drivers, Carl Scarborough, came into the pit and collapsed from heat exhaustion. While he was resting in the pit, some nearby fuel caught fire and he inhaled fumes from the fire extinguishers and passed out. He was taken to the hospital, where he arrived with a temperature of 104 degrees Fahrenheit. He succumbed and died less than two hours after his pit stop.

Q: What fatality struck the German Grand Prix in 1954?

A: During the qualifying round of the 1954 German Grand Prix at Nürburgring, Maserati driver Onofre Marimón lost control of his car on a downhill turn, hitting a ditch, then a tree, flipping several times, and landing upside down. He died shortly after the crash.

Q: What disaster got car racing banned for a time in several European countries?

A: On June 11, 1955, over 250,000 spectators filled the stands at Le Mans, a 24-hour endurance race that is not part of F1, but which has driver crossover with F1. In the third hour of the race at lap 35, Jaguar driver Mike Hawthorn had just passed Austin Healey driver Lance Macklin when he realized he was being called into the pit. He cut across the track and Macklin had to veer to the right and slightly off the track to avoid hitting Hawthorn. When he veered back onto the track, he was in the path of Pierre Levegh's Mercedes. Levegh's front-right tire went up the back of Macklin's Austin Healey, and the Mercedes flew into the air. Levegh was thrown from the car to his death on the track below. The car hit an embankment and debris and fire flew into the stands, killing 83 spectators and injuring hundreds. Controversially, the race was not called off! John Fitch, an American F1 driver who was Levegh's co-driver, convinced Mercedes to withdraw, but the Le Mans runners said that shutting down would cause a mass exodus of spectators that would block emergency vehicles, so the race continued to completion. Several European countries banned all motorsport until better safety precautions could be implemented. The stands at the site of the disaster were demolished and never rebuilt.

Q: What country never lifted their post-Le Mans-disaster racing ban?

A: Switzerland has yet to allow motorsport since the Le Mans disaster.

Q: Which two drivers were killed at the 1955 Indy500?

A: Once again (see above), dual tragedy struck the 1955 Indianapolis 500 competition. First, Manny Ayulo's steering wheel broke and he crashed into a concrete barrier, which took his life the day after. Then a crash occurred in front of Bill Vukovich that he couldn't avoid. His vehicle drove up another car and catapulted over the impact wall, where he slammed into the ground nose first and became engulfed in fire, although it was apparently a broken neck that actually killed him.

Q: What horrible accident caused the 1957 Cuban Grand Prix to be canceled?

A: From 1957 through 1960, three Grands Prix were held in the island nation of Cuba. The weekend of the 1958 Gran Premio de Cuba was both a dramatic affair worthy of world headlines before race day even began and a tragedy in the annals of Formula 1. The drama started when five-time World Champion Juan Manuel Fangio was kidnapped by Fidel Castro's rebels (see Chapter 3 for the off-the-wall details). Despite Fangio being completely missing during the race, the race went on after a delay. The circuit was devoid of barriers, and spectators lined the streets right by the roads as cars were hurtling down at speeds sometimes reaching 160 miles per hour.

During the race, driver Armando Garcia Cifuentes hit an oil slick at a turn on lap six while he was going around 110 miles per hour, slid off the track, and plowed into a crowd of spectators, killing seven and injuring dozens more. Ahead of the race, Fangio had reportedly warned of the danger of this turn and suggested that spectators be moved away from it. The red flag was waved, but the race continued for a few minutes in the confusion. Officials fired shots into the air to keep the crowd back. It was a while before drivers knew what happened.

Q: What fatality struck the 1957 Indy500?

A: During a practice round, Keith Andrews crashed into a wall while going around 136 miles per hour. Like Bill Vukovich two years prior (see above), he suffered a broken neck and died.

Q: What catastrophe led to a fatality in the 1958 Indy500?

A: During the 1958 Indianapolis 500 competition, a 15-car pileup occurred during the very first lap of the race! Pat O'Connor's vehicle catapulted off another car, flipped, and was engulfed in flames. He did not survive.

Q: How were the deaths of Bill Vukovich and Pat O'Connor similar?

A: Motorsport is dangerous and sometimes drivers die in similar ways, like Bill Vukovich and Pat O'Connor, who both lost their lives in the 1955 and 1958 Indianapolis 500 events, respectively, by catapulting off another car, after which their own cars burned on landing. But there were a couple of extra coincidences in the circumstances surrounding their fatal accidents. They also both started in fifth position on the grid. Both were driving blue cars. And both were driving under the driver number 4!

Q: What two Ferrari drivers were killed during the 1958 F1 season just one Grand Prix apart from each other?

A: The first occurred during the French Grand Prix at Reims, where Ferrari driver Luigi Musso, in second place at the time,

lost control on a turn going 150 miles per hour, caught a ditch, and flipped over. He was airlifted by helicopter to a hospital, where he died of his injuries. The second happened at the German Grand Prix at Nürburgring (the very next race weekend after Musso's death), where Peter Collins lost control of his vehicle, ran into a fence, and got thrown from his car into a tree. He suffered a skull fracture and died hours later.

Q: What caused Vanwall team boss Tony Vandervell to withdraw from racing?

A: During the Moroccan Grand Prix in 1958, the engine of Stuart Lewis-Evans's Vanwall locked up, causing him to lose control and crash into a barrier. The car then burst into flames and Lewis-Evans was badly burned. He was transported on Vandervell's private plane to a hospital in England, but he succumbed to his injuries after six days. Vandervell and Bernie Ecclestone were so upset about the loss of their friend that they quit the racing business, Vandervell forever, and Ecclestone for a few years.

Q: What natural occurrence caused the fatal crash of Bob Cortner?

A: During the 1959 Indianapolis 500, driver Bob Cortner lost control of his car when it was caught by a heavy wind that threw it nose-first against a wall. Cortner sustained head injuries that took his life not long after.

Q: What took Harry Schell's life at Silverstone in 1960?

A: During a nonchampionship practice round at Silverstone in England in 1960, wet conditions caused Cooper driver Harry Schell to slide off the road while going around 100 miles per hour. His car flipped and crashed into a brick wall. The wall then fell on him.

Q: What tragedies struck at the 1960 Belgian Grand Prix?

A: At the 1960 Belgian Grand Prix at Spa, there were multiple serious accidents, two of which were fatal. On Friday, Michael Taylor's Lotus steering column broke, causing a crash that paralyzed him. And on Saturday, Stirling Moss crashed and broke both his legs and his nose. Both recovered, although it was a while before Taylor could walk again. Even worse disasters struck during the Sunday race when, first, Cooper driver Chris Bristow lost control in lap 20 and slid into a wire fence that decapitated him. A few laps later, something caused Lotus driver Alan Stacey to lose control of his car. Based on accounts from witnesses, it's possible that his fatal accident was caused by a bird striking him in the face.

Q: What tragedy marred the Italian Grand Prix in 1961?

A: At the Italian Grand Prix at Monza, Ferrari driver Count Wolfgang von Trips collided with Jim Clark's Lotus. Trips's Ferrari flew off the ground and crashed into a fence lined by spectators, throwing him from the vehicle to his death and killing 14 of the spectators. Jim Clark was uninjured but devastated and had to be talked out of retiring after the accident. Clark continued his successful career until 1968, when, during an F2 race at Hockenheim, Germany, he died in a crash caused by a tire blowout.

Q: How was 20-year-old driver Ricardo Rodriquez killed?

A: Ferrari driver Ricardo Rodriguez wanted to drive in the Mexican Grand Prix, but his team decided not to participate in the event, which was nonchampionship and in its first year. So on his own, he entered the race in a Lotus. He took a corner too fast and flipped his car, which caught on fire. He was rushed to the hospital, but sadly he was pronounced dead on arrival.

Q? What fatal accident took the life of Gary Hocking?

A? In the lead up to the 1962 South African Grand Prix, Gary Hocking was practicing for his first F1 race. He had quit motor-cycle racing that same year, thinking car racing would be safer. Unfortunately, he was proven wrong when, during practice, he ran into a ditch and flipped his car, killing him.

Q? What cost Carel Godin de Beaufort his life in the German Grand Prix in 1964?

A? Actually, no one quite knows! For some reason during the 1964 German Grand Prix, Porsche driver Carel Godin de Beaufort's car careened off of the track. He sustained injuries to the head and chest, which took his life three days after.

Q? What injuries took the life of Brabham driver John Taylor?

A? On the very first lap of the 1966 German Grand Prix at Nürburgring, during very wet conditions, John Taylor struck Matra driver Jacky Ickx. Taylor's car caught fire and he sustained heavy burns. Several weeks after the race, he succumbed to his injuries.

Q? What disaster struck at Monaco in 1967?

A? At the 1967 Monaco Grand Prix, Ferrari driver Lorenzo Bandini hit a mooring head and flipped his car at a chicane by the harbor. It slid upside down into bales of straw and burst into flames. He couldn't get out of the burning car right away, and a nearby news helicopter fanned the flames before he was pulled from the vehicle. He sustained chest injuries and heavy burns, to which he succumbed three days after the accident.

Q: What mechanical failure led to Jim Clark's fatal crash?

A: Jim Clark, beloved Scottish racer and record F1 champion for team Lotus in the 1960s, was known to be a careful driver. But while racing an F2 race in Hockenheim Germany in 1968, he had a blowout and crashed fatally.

Q: What experimental car was involved in the death of Jo Schlesser?

A: In 1968, Honda developed an experimental vehicle dubbed the RA302. John Surtees test drove it and declared it unsafe, but it was driven by Jo Schlesser in the 1968 French Grand Prix at Rouen anyway. Sadly, Surtees's review turned out to be right. Just two laps into the race, Schlesser slid sideways and crashed into a bank. The car immediately exploded, killing its driver. Surtees still refused to drive the second RA302 that was built to replace the first one, so Honda pulled out of the season.

Q: What newcomer to F1 had a fatal crash on a test run of an F2 vehicle in 1969?

A: Gerhard Mitter raced a variety of styles and went from motorcycle racing to Formula 1 to sportscar driving and hill-climb, and then back to Formula 1. He had only started five F1 races when BMW asked him to test F2 cars for them, which he did in the lead-up to the 1969 German Grand Prix, in which he was supposed to also drive. On a test run of a BMW F2 car, its suspension failed, and he lost control, crashed, and died.

Q: Which F1 driver was killed at the Dutch Grand Prix in 1970?

A: At the 1970 Dutch Grand Prix at Zandvoort in the Netherlands, De Tomaso driver Piers Courage's car hit a curb, shot up a grass bank, crashed into a fence, and exploded. It was found that a wheel had also come off the car on impact, hit Courage in the cockpit, and knocked his helmet off. The injury from the wheel impact was deemed the most likely cause of his death.

Q: Who is the only F1 driver to have won the Drivers' World Championship posthumously?

A: During the last practice run at the 1970 Italian Grand Prix at Monza, Lotus driver Jochen Rindt crashed into a fence and his car was broken to pieces, but the cause of his death was somewhat unusual. Rindt refused to wear the crotch strap of his car's five-point harness. During his crash, he slid in such a way that the seatbelt crushed his throat. Medics at the on-site infirmary reportedly got his heart beating again, but it stopped, and although they pronounced him dead, they still sent him to the Milan University hospital, where they determined the cause of death. Despite dying before the end of the season, Rindt still had the highest points and became the first and only driver to win the Driver's World Championship posthumously. Rindt was from Germany and held the distinction of being the first non-British driver hired by team Lotus.

Q: What other driver had previously died in the same spot as Jochen Rindt, but years earlier?

A: In the 1961 Italian Grand Prix, Count Wolfgang von Trips fatally crashed in the exact same spot that Jochen Rindt would years later.

Q: What driver death led fellow racer Purley to receive a medal?

A: At the 1973 Dutch Grand Prix, March driver Roger Williamson blew a tire, which caused his car to flip and catch fire. Much like Jo Siffert (see Chapter 4), he could not free himself from the car. Fellow March driver David Purley stopped his car mid-race and ran to Williamson. He heard Williamson crying out for help and tried to get him out of the car, then ran to get a fire extinguisher, ran back, and used it on the flames. The marshals didn't have fire protection and couldn't get close. They eventually pulled Purley away from the fiery scene. A full eight minutes after the crash, a firetruck arrived, but it was far too late. Purley received the George Medal for his valiant attempt to save his fellow driver.

Q: What fatal crash caused Jackie Stewart to quit F1 just before his last race?

A: During qualifying at the 1973 United States Grand Prix in Watkins Glen, New York, Tyrrell driver François Cevert hit a curb and lost control of his car, crashed into unsecured barriers, and flipped over a guardrail. He sustained severe injuries that were deemed to have killed him instantly. Jackie Stewart was one of his teammates, as well as a close friend and mentor to the younger driver. Already having planned to retire after this race, which would have been his hundredth, to make way for young Cevert, Stewart never raced Formula 1 again, but did act as a commentator and continued to advocate for improved safety features in the sport (see Chapter 4). At the time of this writing, Jackie Stewart is still alive and well in Britain.

Q: What driver was killed in the 1974 South African Grand Prix?

A: During a practice run at the 1974 South African Grand Prix, the suspension of British driver Peter "Revvie" Revson's Shadow malfunctioned, and he crashed into the steel guard-rails. This set his car alight and killed him instantly.

Q: What relative of Peter Revson died racing Formula 3?

A: Sadly, Peter wasn't the only Revson to lose his life to racing. Years earlier, in 1967 at a Formula 3 race at the Ring Djursland in Denmark, Doug Revson, younger brother of Peter Revson, had a collision and struck a concrete block, which sent him spinning out of control into a group of officials, including circuit owner Jens Christian Legarth, who was also killed. Five others were injured. Doug Revson died en route to the hospital.

Q: What other victim may have been claimed by unsecured barriers at the track in Watkins Glen?

A: At the 1974 United States Grand Prix at Watkins Glen, New York, Helmuth Koinigg's vehicle had suspension failure and slid under a poorly secured barrier, decapitating him.

Q: What terrible accident at the 1975 Austrian Grand Prix took the life of a driver and a marshal?

A: During a practice run at the 1975 Austrian Grand Prix at Osterreichring, March driver Mark Donahue lost control of his vehicle due to a flat and crashed into a fence, sending debris flying that struck and killed a nearby marshal. Donahue initially survived, but some object (likely a fence post) had caused a brain injury. He went to the hospital due to a bad headache. There he fell into a coma and died. It was discovered that he had suffered a brain hemorrhage.

Q: What accident at the 1977 South African Grand Prix also took the life of a driver and a marshal?

A: At the 1977 South African Grand Prix, Renzo Zorsi had to stop due to engine trouble, and his car caught fire. A pair of marshals walked across the track, one carrying a fire extinguisher, just as driver Hans-Joachim Stuck came around the curve, followed by Tom Pryce. Stuck was able to swerve and miss the marshals, but his car impeded the view of Tom Pryce, who hit the marshal holding the fire extinguisher. The extinguisher flew into Pryce's cockpit, hitting him in the head and killing him. The marshal did not survive, either.

Q: What driver died the next day from injuries sustained in the 1978 Italian Grand Prix?

A: At the 1978 Italian Grand Prix at Monza, a collision led to injuries to both Vittorio Brambilla and Ronnie Peterson. Brambilla suffered head injuries and Peterson suffered leg injuries. It took 15 minutes for an ambulance to arrive due to traffic issues. Brambilla was treated first since a head injury was deemed more of a danger. Peterson was taken to the hospital, and it turned out he had ten leg fractures. They operated, but bone marrow slipped into his bloodstream and caused kidney failure overnight. Peterson passed away the next morning. Brambilla recovered from his injuries.

Q: What fatal accident took the life of Gilles Villeneuve?

A: Ferrari driver Gilles Villeneuve was the older brother of fellow Formula 1 racer Jacques Villeneuve (not to be confused with the younger Jacques Villeneuve, who raced from 1996 to 2006). During a qualifying round at the 1982 Belgian Grand Prix, March driver Jochen Mass, who was driving at a slower pace, moved to the right to allow Villenueve to pass on the left. But Villenueve had already decided to pass on the right. Villeneuve's front left tire hit Mass's back right tire, and Villenueve's Ferrari shot into the air for many meters and crashed to the ground, disintegrating. Villeneuve and his car's seat were thrown together into a fence. He sustained a broken neck and was airlifted to a hospital but did not survive the night.

Q: What driver survived flames but died of wounds from a crash at the 1982 Canadian Grand Prix?

A: At the 1982 Canadian Grand Prix at the newly renamed Circuit Gilles Villeneuve, Osella driver Riccardo Paletti rear-ended Didier Pironi's Ferrari, which had stalled at pole at the start of the race and had caused minor accidents ahead of Paletti's arrival. Pironi was unscathed, but Paletti sustained injuries to his chest. His car burst into flames when the gas tank exploded, but once he was cut out of the car, it was found that he wasn't burned at all due to the fire-resistant driving suit. Unfortunately, his chest injuries were severe, and he succumbed to them at the hospital on the same day.

Q: What two drivers were killed at the San Marino Grand Prix in 1994?

A: Both Simtek driver Roland Ratzenberger and Williams driver Ayrton Senna lost their lives during the 1994 San Marino Grand Prix weekend at the Imola circuit in Italy. During the qualifying round, Ratzenberger damaged his wing on one lap and it broke on the next, causing him to crash into a barrier at 190 miles per hour. The whipping of his head and neck during the crash caused him to sustain a basal skull fracture.

During the next day's race, Senna lost control at a corner and slammed into a concrete crash barrier going approximately 135 miles per hour. He suffered fatal head injuries when debris pierced his helmet. Their deaths led to the Imola circuit adding multiple chicanes to their track and also to FIA's heightened interest in the HANS device, which was eventually made mandatory in 2003. The Simtek team finished the 1994 season after Ratzenberger's death but disbanded afterward.

Q: What was found in Ayrton Senna's car after his crash?

A: Austrian driver Roland Ratzenberger was killed in the qualifying rounds the day before Senna's fatal crash (see above entry for more details of both tragic incidents). An Austrian flag was found in Senna's car after his crash, which he had apparently planned to raise on the podium in honor of Ratzenberger if he won the race.

Q: After the two fatal crashes at the San Marino Grand Prix in 1994, when was the next F1 driver fatality?

A: Jules Bianchi, from Nice, France, suffered a terrible head injury at the 2014 Japanese Grand Prix at Suzuka when he lost control of his car in the rain at 132 miles per hour and crashed into a recovery crane, which had been deployed to retrieve Adrian Suthil's crashed car. Bianchi's car collided with the recovery vehicle in such a way that part of it was underneath the crane, causing Bianchi's helmet to hit the crane. After a thorough investigation, it was reported that the crash subjected him to 254g of g-force. After the crash, Bianchi remained in a coma for nine months until he passed away. This crash resulted in the installation of the virtual safety car (VSC) system.

Q: What former F1 driver was killed in a motorcycle crash the same day as Jules Bianchi's fatal F1 accident?

A: Andrea de Cesaris raced Formula 1 from 1980 to 1994. In 2014, he fatally crashed his motorcycle in Italy. This accident was on the same day that Jules Bianchi crashed into a recovery crane, succumbing to his wounds months later (see entry above).

Q: What female Formula 1 test driver died a little over a year after crashing into an improperly positioned support truck tail lift?

A: Maria de Villota, daughter of former Formula 1 driver Emilio de Villota, was a driver who raced Spanish Formula 3 and sports cars for over a decade before successfully test driving a 2009 Renault R29. This led to a job as a test driver for the Marussia team in 2012. In July, during her first test of one of the team's cars on a straight at Duxford Aerodrome in England, she had issues with locked car controls that made the car fight her instructions as she tried to slow down. She hit the tail lift of a support truck on the way back into the pit that was later deemed to have been left in an unsafe position. Villota lost the use of her right eye but donned an eye patch and seemed to have made a good recovery after multiple operations. But sadly, in October 2013, she passed away at the age of 33 of what were only described by the autopsy as "natural causes."

FLY-BY-NIGHT
SCANDALS AND CONTROVERSIES

Q: Which former team boss did some people believe faked his own death?

A: Car engineer, founder of British company Lotus Cars, and former Lotus Cars team principal Colin Chapman was under investigation due to his dealings with car manufacturer John Zachary DeLorean. DeLorean rose from engineer to executive at GM and then started his own company, DeLorean Motor Company. DeLorean enlisted Lotus Cars to provide additional design and engineering work for the DeLorean DMC-12 (a stainless-steel rear-engine gull-winged sports car most famous for its conversion into a time machine by Doc Brown in the 1985 film *Back to the Future*), initially designed by Giorgetto Giugiaro.

DeLorean received around 85 million pounds from the British government to subsidize the creation of a factory in Northern Ireland to manufacture the vehicle. When he was arrested at LAX for drug trafficking in 1982 (a charge for which he was later acquitted), monetary irregularities came to light during the investigation, revealing that he had squandered 10 million pounds (around $16 million dollars at the time) of the money from the British government. About $5 million went to Lotus Cars via offshore bank accounts created by Chapman and Lotus Cars chair Fred Bushell. Bushell was ultimately sentenced to five years. Chapman was facing a possible 10-year sentence, but in 1982, before he went to trial, he died of a heart attack at the young age of 54.

F1 aerodynamics engineer Adrian Newey claimed in his autobiography that F1 driver Mario Andretti said that Chapman faked his death and escaped his legal troubles by fleeing to Brazil, although Andretti himself would not corroborate this and there is reportedly little evidence to support the assertion. But that hasn't stopped the conspiracy theory of Chapman's faked death from persisting.

Q: What driver was famously asked to let his Ferrari teammate pass him?

A: Ferrari driver Rubens Barrichello was told by his team to let his teammate Michael Schumacher pass him not once, but twice! During the 2001 Formula 1 season, Barrichello was asked over the radio to let Schumacher pass him so that Schumacher could win his fourth Drivers' World Championship. As a result, Barichello came in third behind Schumacher in second. In 2002, during the Austrian Grand Prix at the A1-Ring in Spielberg, Austria, Barichello was in the lead for the whole race, but he was told once again, and on the last turn of the last lap, to let Schumacher pass so that he could win the race. Schumacher won the World Championship that year, as well as the next two.

Q: What F1 scandal was dubbed "Spygate?"

A: In 2007, an act of industrial espionage shook the F1 world. Ferrari chief mechanic Nigel Stepney handed over around 800 pages of documents to McLaren chief designer Mike Coughlan. Coughlan had his wife take the documents to be photocopied. The shop in England that did the photocopying reported the contents, and an investigation was opened. Ferrari suspended Stepney and sued Coughlan. The FIA fined the McLaren team $100 million and disqualified them from the Constructors' Championship, which they would have won. The McLaren drivers were still allowed to compete and keep their points. It was never found that any of Ferrari's designs were actually incorporated into McLaren's car designs.

Q: What was Crashgate in F1?

A: At the 2008 Singapore Grand Prix, Renault driver Fernando Alonso had technical difficulties during the second qualifying round that left him fifteenth in the lineup at the start of the race. At lap 12, he made the first pit stop of the race and rejoined at the back. During lap 14, his teammate Nelson Piquet, Jr,. crashed into a wall at the seventeenth turn, a spot that meant the safety car would need to be deployed. Alonso was able to move up and managed to come in first in the race. It was chalked up to luck due to the timing of the safety car, and the world of F1 moved on. That is, until Piquet was let go by the Renault team in 2009 and he spilled his guts about his crash being a setup. He alleged that Renault managing director Flavio Briatore and director of engineering Pat Symonds had ordered him to crash when and where he did on purpose to give Alonso a shot at the lead. Symonds confessed and got a five-year ban from F1 and FIA events, while Briatore was banned indefinitely, and the Renault team was banned from the sport for two years. Alonso was cleared of involvement in the scheme. Symonds's and Briatore's bans were overturned by a French court, but as part of a settlement during appeal, Symonds and Briatore agreed not to work in F1 until 2013 and any other FIA event until late 2011.

Q: What controversial new points scheme was introduced in 2014 and abandoned immediately after?

A: Before the 2014 Formula 1 season, Bernie Ecclestone suggested awarding double points in the last three races of the season to make the stakes higher and bring in viewers. The FIA decided to award double points in only the last Grand Prix of the season in Abu Dhabi. The new rule was unpopular with drivers and fans alike and only lasted one season. In 2015 and all subsequent seasons, Formula 1 stuck with the usual points system.

Q: What former F1 magnate was found guilty of tax fraud?

A: Bernie Ecclestone, sometimes referred to as the "F1 supremo" and whose long career in Formula 1 included a short stint as a driver, ownership of the Brabham team, and the founding of the Formula 1 group, pled guilty after he was caught lying to authorities about offshore accounts. In October 2023, he was ordered to pay back taxes and received a suspended prison sentence of 17 months.

Q: What team's car design caused speculation and controversy during the 2020 F1 season?

A: Racing Point (formerly Force India until it was bought and rebranded by Lawrence Stroll) did a major redesign for their 2020 car. When it was first taken out during winter practice, there was a lot of chatter that it looked a lot like the Mercedes design that had done so well the previous season, and the new Racing Point vehicle also managed to get the best time during practice. This led to speculation that they may have copied Mercedes's designs a bit too closely for legality. Racing Point insisted that while they had been inspired by aspects of the winning Mercedes, everything they did to build their new car was perfectly within the rules of Formula 1.

Q: What team was deemed to have gone over the allowed budget in 2021?

A: After an investigation, the FIA determined that Red Bull Racing went over the allowed budget by around half a million dollars for the 2021 season. But it was only after taking into account an unclaimed $1.6 million dollar tax credit that investigators found that there was no intent to breach the budget cap rule. Despite that, Red Bull was fined $7 million and the amount of time they were allowed wind tunnel testing for the next season was decreased by 10 percent.

Q: What referee decision in the final 2021 Grand Prix was deemed an error after the fact and likely may have changed the outcome of the race and the World Championship?

A: At the start of the 2021 Abu Dhabi Grand Prix, reigning champion Lewis Hamilton and Max Verstappen were tied for points. Verstappen took pole position but was passed by Lewis Hamilton, who spent most of the race in the lead. Near the end of the race, Williams driver Nicholas Latifi had a crash, and a safety car was deployed. Mercedes didn't have Hamilton pit for new tires, but Red Bull Racing pitted Verstappen. F1 race manager Michael Masi made a call to let the five lapped drivers between Hamilton, who was in first place, and Verstappen, who was in second place, unlap themselves (but, unusually, not the other lapped cars). So, when the race resumed, Verstappen started right behind Hamilton, with just one lap to go in the race. With his new fresh tires, Verstappen overtook Hamilton, winning both the Grand Prix and the World Champion title that Hamilton had held for the previous four years. To say the least, Hamilton and Mercedes were upset by the unorthodox restart decision and the outcome of the last lap of the race. Mercedes appealed several times, and although Masi's decision to start the race back in such a manner was ultimately ruled a mistake, the results were not overturned, and Verstappen remained World Champion for 2021. In a year that Hamilton was poised to possibly beat the record for most World Championship wins in Formula 1 (a record he is still tied for with Michael Schumacher at seven World Championships each), instead Verstappen won his first. Masi was let go after the debacle. Max Verstappen has now won the World Championship in 2021, 2022, and 2023.

Q: What prompted the FIA president to step down from day-to-day F1 duties?

A: FIA president Mohammed Ben Sulayem had a disagreement with Liberty Media (which bought Formula 1's commercial entity) because Sulayem wanted to add a new team, and perhaps expand to 12 teams. He also stated that Formula 1 was not worth the $20 billion rumored value.

Q: What comment on an old website of FIA president stirred controversy?

A: In January 2023, a comment from the current FIA president Mohammed Ben Sulayem surfaced from an archived version of his own website, on which he reportedly stated in 2001 that he didn't like "women who are smarter than men, for they are not in truth." Sulayem denies accusations of misogyny, citing his hiring of Natalie Robyn, the first female FIA CEO, as well as other female staff, and creating an equity, diversity, and inclusion (EDI) commission.

Q: What company became a short-lived sponsor of the Haas team?

A: Rich Energy, an energy drink company helmed at the time by CEO William Storey and incorporated in Britain in 2015 (a rebranding of a Croatian company, Rich, that launched in 2011), became the title sponsor of the Haas team during the 2019 season. The beverage company's name, logo, and black and gold colors emblazoned the team's car and uniforms. But the sponsorship, and maybe even the company itself, wasn't all it was cracked up to be. Rich Energy first approached the Force India Team, then Williams, before becoming the Haas sponsor. Controversy was stirred when it was discovered that in 2017, only two years prior, the company had 581 pounds (less than $800) in its bank account.

Storey dismissed concerns and said that the company had plenty of money. The company taunted Red Bull, the dominant rival energy drink company that has its own F1 team, via the official Rich Energy Twitter account. Midway through the F1 season, British company Whyte Bikes sued Rich Energy for having too similar a logo. Rich Energy was barred from using the logo and it was removed from the Haas car. Just before the British Grand Prix at Silverstone, the official Rich Energy Twitter account announced that the company had terminated its sponsorship of the Haas team due to the team's poor performance. Rich Energy shareholders released a statement that the tweet was the work of a "rogue individual."

Further tweets over the race weekend disparaged the Haas team and referenced a coup going on in the drink company. Storey was ousted from the company and its name was changed to Lightning Volt the day after the British Grand Prix. The Haas team acknowledged the end of the sponsorship in September 2019. The team had reportedly only received an initial payment from the company and not the entire $60 million of expected sponsorship money.

Q: What incident got both Max Verstappen and Daniel Ricciardo reprimanded at the 2018 Azerbaijan Grand Prix?

A: During the 2018 Azerbaijan Grand Prix in Baku, Red Bull Racing teammates Daniel Ricciardo and Max Verstappen were in a battle, not just against the other teams' drivers, but against each other. They touched wheels and passed each other a couple of times. But around lap 40, Ricciardo slammed into the back of Verstappen during an attempt to pass, ending the race for both of them. The stewards ruled that both had made moves that contributed to the incident, Ricciardo in his attempt to pass and Verstappen in his attempts to block him. Both drivers were reprimanded, and both apologized. The reprimands were their first of the season and therefore didn't affect their ability to race the rest of the season, although losing the race and missing out on potentially scoring over 20 points for their team was likely punishment enough. Ricciardo left Red Bull Racing at the end of the 2018 season.

Q: What F1 team owner fought extradition on financial fraud charges?

A: In 2007, Indian businessman Vijay Mallya, owner of Kingfisher Airlines, bought Formula 1 team Spyker, which became Force India for the 2008 season. Mallya faced financial and legal difficulties after his airline went under in 2012. In 2016, he moved to England and left over $1 billion in unpaid debt behind. India attempted to extradite him for fraud. In 2017, he garnered a contempt conviction for transferring $40 million to his kids, assets that he apparently failed to disclose after defaulting on loans related to his airline. He continued to run Force India until 2018, when the team went into administration amid revelations that it had sustained around a $372 million net loss and was over $37 million in debt to over 450 creditors. The team was then bought by Lawrence Stroll, who had previously been a financial backer of Williams, for whom his son Lance Stroll raced. Force India was rebranded as Racing Point in 2019, and then as Aston Martin in 2021. In 2022, Mallya received a four-month sentence in India for his contempt charge, but as of 2023, Mallya remained in London fighting extradition to India.

Q: What FIA attempt to reduce controversy is in and of itself controversial?

A: In 2023, the FIA made a new rule that drivers could not speak out on personal, religious, or political matters during a Grand Prix weekend without either being prompted by a press question or given permission beforehand. Breaking the rule can result in a race penalty. Hamilton, known for his social activism, expressed disapproval over the new rule.

CHAPTER 14

JOYRIDES
POP CULTURE AND FUN FACTS

ℚ𝓈 What Formula 1 driver became a television and movie director?

𝒜𝓈 Formula 1 driver Bruce Kessler made the jump from Formula 1 racing to directing in 1962 with a documentary short film called "The Sound of Speed" that shows driver Lance Reventlow at work driving a Formula 1 Scarab. From that close-to-home project, Kessler went on to earn 68 director credits on popular television series like *The Monkees*, *Mission: Impossible*, *Knight Rider*, and *MacGyver*, as well as a number of made-for-TV movies.

ℚ𝓈 Which Formula 1 superstar's dog has a successful Instagram account?

𝒜𝓈 British driver Lewis Hamilton's bulldog Roscoe Hamilton has nearly a million Instagram followers. Roscoe has also appeared in advertising for the Zapp grocery delivery service with his owner.

ℚ𝓈 What F1 rivalry was the 2013 Ron Howard film *Rush* based on?

𝒜𝓈 The 2013 film *Rush*, directed by Ron Howard, is a biopic about the 1970s Formula 1 rivalry between Niki Lauda (played by Daniel Bruhl) and James Hunt (played by Chris Hemsworth).

ℚ𝓈 What Netflix documentary series showcases Formula 1 racing?

𝒜𝓈 The Netflix series *Formula 1: Drive to Survive* has run from 2019 to the present. It follows the 10 teams as they compete their way through a season of Formula 1 each television season. It gives the viewer an intimate behind-the-scenes look at the sport, the crew, and the drivers, although it's not without its controversy. Some past participants have announced that they will no longer give interviews on the show because they feel it plays up the rivalries a bit too much for dramatic effect.

Q: What upcoming movie about Formula 1 was filmed in part at the 2023 British Grand Prix at Silverstone?

A: Filming for a movie whose title on IMDb is only listed as *Untitled Formula One Racing Movie*, but whose title has been referred to elsewhere as *Apex* (whether that is a working title or the actual theatrical title remains to be seen) took place at the 2023 British Grand Prix weekend at Silverstone Circuit in England. The film stars Brad Pitt, an avid racing fan, as a former Formula 1 racer who comes back to mentor a young driver. It was filmed in part at the Grand Prix, where the fake movie team had a garage between Ferrari and Mercedes. The film is slated for 2024 release but may be pushed back to 2025 due to the recent SAG-AFTRA strikes. The strikes also meant that planned shooting at the Las Vegas Grand Prix in November 2023 had to be canceled. Formula 1 seven-time World Champion Lewis Hamilton is a producer on the project and will make an appearance in the film.

Q: What episode of *Midsomer Murders* references Formula 1 racing?

A: Season 14, episode 1, called "Death in the Slow Lane," of the British detective series Midsomer Murders was the first one where DCI John Barnaby (Neil Dudgeon) takes over for his recently retired cousin Tom Barnaby (John Nettles). The episode begins with fictionalized footage of the 1950 British Grand Prix at Silverstone as the time and place of the first official Formula

1 championship race. Unfortunately for the fictional driver, the plot includes the discovery of his body (still in the car) years later. Not much of a spoiler since it happens right after the race footage.

Q: What was the first video game to feature a real racetrack?

A: Namco released two early Formula 1 racing games, the first in 1976 entitled F-1, and the second in 1982 entitled Pole Position. The track in Pole Position was based on the Fuji Speedway, a real racetrack (or as close as they could get to it with 1982 game graphics) in Japan that was used for several Japanese Grands Prix in the 1970s and in the early 2000s.

Q: What whimsical trophy was the result of a gaming company sponsorship of a team and Grand Prix?

A: Sega had two Formula 1 games under their belt by 1992: Super Monaco GP in 1978 and Ayrton Senna's Super Monaco GP II in 1992. But in 1993, they took F1 and gaming crossover marketing to a new level. Sega became the title sponsor for both the Williams team and the 1993 European Grand Prix, renamed the XXXVIII Sega European Grand Prix. The entire circuit was emblazoned with Sega and Sonic-related spectacles: a large monitor shaped like a Sega Game Gear, a huge inflatable Sonic the Hedgehog, performers dressed as Sonic, Sega billboards and banners lining the track, and even Sonic the Hedgehog legs painted on the sides of the Williams cars to look like they were hitting the pedals.

On the rainy race day, McLaren driver Ayrton Senna took the lead, lapped all but one other racer, and came in over a minute before his second-place rival! It was a memorable enough day with that stellar drive alone. But in a marketing piece de resis-

tance, Senna lifted a huge Sonic the Hedgehog trophy at the podium. He was reportedly given the traditional one later, and the Sonic trophy is still with the McLaren team and is still a thing of legend in gaming and F1 circles.

Q: What modern realistic game lets you simulate F1 driving?

A: EA Sports F1 series (originally by Codemasters) are increasingly realistic race games and make you feel like you are in the cockpit of your own Formula 1 vehicle, pulling into the pit lane, and racing against a sea of rival teams and drivers. It even keeps up with changes like the new Sprint races. Over 20 have been put out to date, the latest F1 23.

Q: What were the book and movie *Chitty Chitty Bang Bang* named for?

A: Chitty Chitty Bang Bang is the name of a 1964 book and 1968 film adaptation (written by Roald Dahl) about a flying car that took the protagonists on an adventure. The title was actually lifted from the name of an actual racing car manufactured by Paragon Motor Company, rebuilt for racing by Caractacus Pott, and driven by Count Louis Zborowski in the 1920s.

Q: What famous Hollywood actor drove a modern F1 car?

A: Although Tom Cruise never raced Formula 1, he did drive an F1 car around Willow Springs International Raceway in California in 2011. Known for doing his own stunts, including motorbike and car stunts, he got the car up to 181 miles per hour and received praise from the crew for his skills.

Ⓠ What trio of celebrities invested in a Formula 1 team in 2023?

Ⓐ Actors Michael B. Jordan, Rob McElhenney, and Ryan Reynolds joined a group of investors who made a deal to acquire a stake in the Alpine racing team, the team formerly known as Renault (Renault is the parent company of the car company Société des Automobiles Alpine SAS, aka Alpine).

Ⓠ Which celebrity is married to Red Bull Racing team boss Christian Horner?

Ⓐ Geri Halliwell (now Geri Halliwell-Horner) and Christian Horner married. Halliwell-Horner is an author, a musician, and former member of the British pop sensation the Spice Girls. The pair met at the 2009 Monaco Grand Prix, began dating in 2014, and got married in 2015. They have one child together and two from previous relationships. Her YA novel *Rosie Frost and the Falcon Queen* came out in October 2023. She has also appeared in the Netflix documentary series *Formula 1: Drive to Survive* with her husband.

Ⓠ What F1 boss signed the gamer turned racer on whom the movie *Gran Turismo* is based?

Ⓐ In 2011, Jann Mardenborough famously zoomed to the top of the GT Academy competition held by Sony (the maker of the Gran Turismo video game based on the real racing series) and Nissan to take a Gran Turismo gamer from simulated driving to real racing. The GT Academy combined several weeks of Gran Turismo 5–simulated driving with actual race trials until four contenders were picked to race each other at Silverstone. Mardenborough won and was trained for 6 months to help him

achieve his international license. He has since competed in a number of racing series, some sportscar and some Formula. And in 2014, famous F1 Red Bull Racing team boss Christian Horner signed him on for the 2014 GP3 series season to race with the Arden International team. In 2023, Mardenborough's story was dramatized by the film Gran Turismo, with Archie Madekwe as Mardenborough and Christian Horner's wife Geri Halliwell as Mardenborough's mum.

Q: What sponsorship turned the 2005 Monaco Grand Prix into a galactic event?

A: The day after the release of 2005 movie *Star Wars: Revenge of the Sith*, Star Wars characters, branding, and even costumes took over the Red Bull Racing team for the 2005 Monaco Grand Prix weekend. Director George Lucas, Anakin actor Hayden Christiensen, and the Emperor actor Ian McDiarmid were in attendance. Darth Vader, R2D2, C3P0, Chewbacca, and a bunch of Stormtroopers cheered (or menaced) from the sidelines, the cars were covered in Star Wars skins, and the Red Bull Racing pit crew's uniforms were custom-made to resemble Clone Troopers from the prequels (as closely as they could while still maintaining safety standards, of course). The force was with McLaren's Kimi Raikkonen, who took first place, followed by Nick Heidfeld in second, and Mark Webber in third.

Q: What clothing company once owned a Formula 1 team?

A: In 1984, the Toleman team was bought by the clothing company Benetton, and the team was rebranded as the Benetton Formula 1 Team. It ran until 1999, when the team was purchased by Renault. The Benetton F1 team even managed to win the 1994 and 1995 driver World Championships via one of their drivers at the time: seven-time World Champion Michael Schumacher. They actually aren't the only clothing line whose name has been featured on a Formula 1 team. Red Bull Racing's junior team was (until 2024) named AlphaTauri, which was the name of Red Bull's own clothing line.

Q: What inanimate object racing on YouTube gained viewers during the pandemic?

A: During the start of the deadly COVID-19 coronavirus pandemic in early 2020, most sporting events were canceled to help prevent the spread of the virus, and fans needed something to watch. Many athletes made online videos creatively displaying their skills, but these weren't quite the same as viewing a competitive sporting event. One whimsical online sport that gained viewers during this extreme dearth of events was marble racing!

YouTube channel *Jelle's Marble Runs* (@JellesMarbleRuns), based in the Netherlands and pronounced "yell-ehs," posted their first video, a Sand Marble Rally, on November 13, 2018, where seven marbles with names like Crazy Cat's Eye and Comet raced down a circuit dug out in the sand to a finish line replete with a banner while a sports color commentator described the race as it went. Over time, the videos became more intricate, with innovative track construction for various sorts of marble races and stands full of marble spectators. In 2019, the marble runs were featured on ESPN8's *The Ocho* program. In February 2020, they began staging Marbula One races, including both qualifying rounds and GPs. The channel had already gained a sizable viewership of half a million by early 2020, but their popularity ballooned to over a million after the outbreak.

In at least one video during the pandemic, the marbles in the stands were wearing little masks! John Oliver featured them on *Last Week Tonight* and sponsored the Marble League, after which the circuits featured *Last Week Tonight* sponsorship banners. Marbula 1 and other racing competition videos are still being produced and posted regularly as of this writing.

Q: What team principal got a tattoo to fulfill a challenge and to commemorate a team win?

A: The Grand Prix Trust charity has an Industry Leaders' Challenge, where each year a team boss sets a challenge for another team boss to do something that scares them. Mercedes team boss Toto Wolff challenged McLaren team boss Zak Brown, who is afraid of needles, to get a tattoo. He didn't get it right away, but fate intervened at the 2021 Italian Grand Prix at Monza when McClaren drivers Daniel Ricciardo and Lando Norris took first and second places! Brown got a tattoo of the Monza circuit to commemorate the victory.

CONCLUSION

The history and universe of motorsports is an adrenaline-fueled thrill ride punctuated by times of great tragedy. And Formula 1 sits at the pinnacle of all aspects of the sport. The incredible innovation that goes into the world's most sophisticated and aerodynamic cars, the back-breaking labor that goes into the preparation for and execution of the races, and the incredible skills of drivers going faster than almost any other terrestrial beings is addictive. This book has hundreds of entries and still only manages to scratch the surface. There is so much more to know, and hopefully so much more in store for us fans to see in the future of the sport. May all your F1 dreams come true.

REFERENCES

ABB Formula E. "Formula E and FIA Reveal All-Electric Gen3 Race Car in Monaco." April 28, 2022. https://www.fiaformulae.com/en/news/2456/formula-e-and-fia-reveal-all-electric-gen3-race-car-in-monaco.

AMG Petronas Formula One Team. "F1 Explained: How Each of the Iconic Monaco GP Corners Got Its Name." Accessed May 28, 2024. https://www.mercedesamgf1.com/news/f1-explained-how-each-of-the-iconic-monaco-gp-corners-got-its-name.

Andretti Autosport. "About the Team." Accessed February 11, 2024. https://andrettiautosport.com/about.

Andretti, Mario. "Time 100 Icons—Lewis Hamilton." *Time*. April 21, 2016. https://time.com/collection-post/4298226/lewis-hamilton-2016-time-100.

Arron, Simon. "Moss' Landmark 1958 Argentine GP Victory." *Motorsport*. April 16, 2018. https://www.motorsportmagazine.com/articles/single-seaters/f1/moss-landmark-1958-argentine-gp-victory.

Arroyo, Juan. "Behind the Wheel: Breaking Down Each Junior Series Car on the FIA Ladder." Feeder Series. Last updated September 29, 2023. https://feederseries.net/2023/09/18/behind-the-wheel-breaking-down-each-junior-series-car.

Asher, Richard. "F1 Team Principals: Who Are They and What Do They Do?" Motorsport.com. August 9, 2022. https://us.motorsport.com/f1/news/f1-team-principals-who-are-they-and-what-do-they-do/10351168.

Aston Martin F1. "The Race for F1 Safety: The Six-Point Seatbelt." April 10, 2021. https://www.astonmartinf1.com/en-GB/news/feature/the-race-for-f1-safety-the-six-point-seatbelt.

The Athletic. "F1 Live News: Mercedes Won't Appeal Abu Dhabi Result, Will Push for Changes; Verstappen Remains F1 Champion; Hamilton's F1 Future Questioned." December 16, 2021. https://theathletic.com/live-blogs/abu-dhabi-grand-prix-f1-championship-lewis-hamilton-and-max-verstappen/g6dO0HIceqOJ/?redirected=1.

Autosport. "F1 Driver Jobs before Formula 1—Raikkonen, Mansell, Webber, & More." September 7, 2020. https://www.autosport.com/f1/news/f1-driver-jobs-before-formula-1-raikkonen-mansell-webber-more-4979332/4979332.

Autosport. "Maria de Villota Obituary: 1980–2013." October 11, 2013. https://www.autosport.com/f1/news/maria-de-villota-obituary-1980-2013-4468879/4468879.

Baime, A. J. "The Lasting Legacy of Formula 1's Tragic Hero Francois Cevert." *Road and Track*. October 13, 2023. https://www.roadandtrack.com/car-culture/a45458472/the-lasting-legacy-of-formula-1s-tragic-hero-francois-cevert.

Balfour, Andrew. "Race Facts—French Grand Prix." F1 Destinations. July 26, 2022. https://f1destinations.com/race-facts-french-grand-prix.

Balla, Elyssa. "F1 G-Force: How Many G's Can a F1 Car Pull?" F1 Chronicle. September 9, 2023. https://f1chronicle.com/f1-g-force-how-many-gs-can-a-f1 -car-pull.

Bandini, Nicky. "Malaysian Grand Prix—As It Happened!" *The Guardian*. April 5, 2009. https://www.theguardian.com/sport/2009/apr/05/formulaone-motor sports.

Barreto, Lawrence. "Maria de Villota's 2023 Marussia F1 Test Crash Details Explained." Autosport. June 29, 2015. https://www.autosport.com/f1/news /maria-de-villotas-2012-marussia-f1-test-crash-details-explained-5004855 /5004855.

BAT. "British American Tobacco announces enhanced partnership with McLaren Racing." November 29, 2019. https://www.bat.com/media/press-releases /_2019/november/nov-29—british-american-tobacco-announces-enhanced -partnership.

BBC Sport. "Maria De Villota: F1 Reserve Driver Died of 'Natural Causes' in Spain." October 11, 2013. https://www.bbc.com/sport/formula1/24487701.

Beer, Matt. "Every Last-to-First Win in Formula 1 History." The Race. December 9, 2020. https://www.the-race.com/formula-1/every-last-to-first-win-in-formula -1-history.

Bekking, Casper. "F1 Reserve Drivers: All the Back-Up Racers for 2023." Motorsport.com. July 18, 2023. https://us.motorsport.com/f1/news/f1 -reserve-drivers-all-teams-backup-2023/10437682.

Bellingham, Tom. "6 People You Never Knew Drove F1 Cars." Red Bull. August 2, 2016. https://www.redbull.com/us-en/unusual-f1-stars-list.

Benson, Andrew. "Anthoine Hubert Fatal Crash Report Finds No Single Cause and No-One to Blame." BBC. February 7, 2020. https://www.bbc.com/sport /motorsport/51415685.

Benson, Andrew. "Japanese Grand Prix : Memories of Jules Bianchi Death Trigger Anger over Recovery Truck on Track." BBC. October 9, 2022. https://www.bbc.com/sport/formula1/63190448.

Biswas, Sabyasachi. "How Do F1 Drivers Lose Weight During a Race?" Essentially Sports. January 25, 2023. https://www.essentiallysports.coms/f1 -news-how-do-f1-drivers-lose-weight-during-a-race.

BMW. "The Woman with the Formula for Racetracks." January 9, 2021. https://www.bmw.com/en/automotive-life/vanessa-mientus-and-the-formula -for-racetracks.html.

"Box, Box | The Pit Stop Explained." Mercedes AMG F1. Accessed January 28, 2024. https://www.mercedesamgf1.com/news/box-box-pitstop-explained.

Boxall-Legge, Jake. "The Biggest Incidents of F1 Cheating: Spygate, Crashgate and More." Motorsport.com. August 4, 2023. https://us.motorsport.com/f1 /news/f1-cheating-spygate-crashgate/6555687.

Bradley, Charles. "Motorsport Heroes: Massa Recalls the Day He Almost Died." Motorsport.com. June 16, 2020. https://us.motorsport.com/f1/news/felipe -massa-almost-died-hungary-ferrari/4793814.

Braybrook, Rebecca. "Which Country Has Hosted the Most F1 Races? Tracks with the Most Grands Prix." Motorsport.com. January 4, 2024. https://www.motorsport.com/f1/news/which-country-hosted-most-f1-races/10560961.

Brisse, Morgan and Christopher Muscato. "Venturi Effect | Definition, Equation & Applications." Study.com. Last updated November 21, 2023. https://study.com/academy/lesson/the-venturi-effect-and-blood-flow.html.

Brittle, Cian. "F1 gets FIA Approval for 2026 Engine Regulations." Blackbook Motorsport. August 17, 2022. https://www.blackbookmotorsport.com/news/f1-fia-approval-2026-engine-regulations-porsche-audi.

Brooklands Museum. "Our History—Timeline." Accessed January 13, 2024. https://www.brooklandsmuseum.com/explore/heritage-and-collection/timeline.

Brownell, Bradley. "It's Irresponsible for Formula 1 to Make Drivers Race on 100-Degree Days." Jalopnik. October 10, 2023. https://jalopnik.com/its-negligent-for-formula-1-to-make-drivers-race-on-100-1850914273.

"Bruce Kessler." IMDb. Accessed February 12, 2024. https://www.imdb.com/name/nm0450314/?ref_=tt_cl_dr_1.

Bullen, Vivien. "What Is a Stock Car?" HowStuffWorks. Accessed February 3, 2024. https://auto.howstuffworks.com/auto-racing/nascar/nascar-basics/stock-car.htm.

Champions—The Speakers Agency. "Sir Jackie Stewart—Former F1 Racing Driver, C X World Drivers' Championship Winner Inducted into the Motorsport Hall of Fame." Accessed February 11, 2024. https://champions-speakers.co.uk/speaker-agent/jackie-stewart.

Clash, Jim. "Surviving 3 Laps in a 2-Seat McLaren F-1 Car, Courtesy of Mika Hakkinen." *Forbes*. November 14, 2021. https://www.forbes.com/sites/jimclash/2021/11/14/surviving-3-laps-in-a-2-seat-mclaren-f-1-car-courtesy-of-mika-hakkinen/?sh=5da58fe65387.

Cobb, Haydn. "What Is F1's Summer Break, Why Does It Happen, and How Long Is It?" Motorsport.com. August 8, 2023. https://us.motorsport.com/f1/news/what-is-f1-summer-break-why-does-it-happen-how-long/10346925.

Coch, Mat. "All F1 2024 Team Bosses." Speedcafe. January 16, 2024. https://speedcafe.com/all-f1-team-bosses.

Coleman, Madeline. "F1's 107 Percent Rule: How Logan Sargeant's Saudia Arabia Weekend Almost Derailed." *New York Times*. March 27, 2023. https://www.nytimes.com/athletic/4352639/2023/03/27/107-percent-rule-formula-one.

Coleman, Madeline. "What Is Porpoising, and Has F1 Made It Extinct for 2023?" *The Athletic*. February 4, 2023.

Colin Chapman Museum. "Delorean." Accessed January 21, 2024. http://www.colinchapmanmuseum.co.uk/?page_id=2351.

Collins, Jason and Kurt Spurlock. "From F1 to Drag Racing: Here's a Breakdown of All the Major Types of Car Racing." The Manual. July 31, 2023. https://www.themanual.com/auto/types-of-car-racing.

Cooper, Adam. "Andretti Cadillac Challenges Key F1 Rejection Claims." Motorsports.com. February 6, 2024. https://www.motorsport.com/f1/news/f1-andretti-cadillac-challenges-key-rejection-claims/10571888.

Cooper, Adam. "The Inside Story of Villenueve's Final F1 Weekend." Motorsports
.com. May 8, 2021. Last updated May 8, 2023. https://us.motorsport.com/f1
/news/gilles-villeneuve-ferrari-death-zolder/4789836.

Cooper, George. "Formula One's Forgotten Gay Pioneer." LGBTQ Nation. August
25, 2022. https://www.lgbtqnation.com/2022/08/formula-ones-forgotten-gay
-pioneer.

Cooper, Sam. "Lewis Hamilton Will Regret Supporting Black Lives Matter
According to An F1 Boss Who Ran the Sport for Decades." *Business Insider*.
July 15, 2021. https://www.businessinsider.com/bernie-ecclestone-criticizes
-lewis-hamiltons-support-of-black-lives-matter-2021-7.

Craig, Christopher. "Shock and Awesome: The 10 Most Memorable Formula One
Moments." *Bleacher Report*. September 29, 2010. https://syndication
.bleacherreport.com/amp/476873-shock-and-awe-formula-ones-ten-most
-memorable-moments.amp.html.

Craig, Jenny. "Schumacher Reveals Main Reason Why He LOST Out to Brother
Michael." GP Fans. August 16, 2023. https://www.gpfans.com/en/f1-news
/1001722/michael-schumacher-ralf-f1-rivalry-luck/#.

Crash. "Vijay Mallya: Ex-Force India Owner Jailed over $40M Payment Linked to
Failed Airline." July 13, 2022. https://www.crash.net/f1/news/1007898/1
/exforce-india-owner-vijay-mallya-jailed-over-40m-payment.

Crebolder, Finley. "Wolff's Challenge the Reason Brown Got Tattoo." PlanetF1.
October 29, 2021. https://www.planetf1.com/news/toto-wolff-zak-brown-tattoo.

Crisara, Matt. "Formula 1's Best Circuits: Past and Present." *Popular Mechanics*.
May 18, 2022. https://www.popularmechanics.com/cars/g40022274/best
-formula-1-circuits.

DeGroote, Steven. "Formula One regulations." F1 Technical. August 2, 2013.
https://www.f1technical.net/articles/20.

De Groote, Steven. "Preparing the Carbon Fibres." F1 Technical. December 15,
2003.

Duncan, Lewis. "Miller: 2016 Dutch TT 'Shoey' Was a "Dig" at Honda."
Motorsport.com. April 26, 2020. https://us.motorsport.com/motogp/news
/miller-shoey-assen-honda-dig/4784705.

DuPont. "Nomex Fibers." Accessed September 10, 2023. https://www.dupont
.com/products/nomex-fibers.html#.

Duxbury, Anna. "F1 vs IndyCar: Which Is Faster, Horsepower, Assists, and More
Compared." Motorsport.com. Last updated May 22, 2023. https://us
.motorsport.com/indycar/news/f1-vs-indycar-which-faster/6512721.

Duxbury, Anna. "History of Safety Devices in Formula 1: The Halo, Barriers
& More." July 4, 2022. Autosport. https://www.autosport.com/f1/news/history
-of-safety-devices-in-formula-1-the-halo-barriers-more-4982360/4982360.

Dymock, Eric. "From the Vault: Motor Racing Legend Graham Hill Killed in a
Plane Crash." *The Guardian (Classic)*. December 2, 2008.
https://www.theguardian.com/sport/blog/2008/dec/02/from-the-vault-graham
-hill-formula-one.

EA Games. "Be the Last to Brake in EA SPORTS F1 23." Accessed February 12,
2024.

EA Sports F1. "F1 22 | Features Trailer." May 31, 2022. https://www.youtube.com
/watch?v=YgOi41qmlc4.

Elshebiny, Yara. "F1 Explained: How Does Points Scoring System Work?" GP
Fans. November 19, 2023. https://www.gpfans.com/en/f1-news/1007641
/f1-points-system.

Elson, James. "How Much Does an F1 Car Cost?" *MotorSport Magazine*. May
21, 2021. https://www.motorsportmagazine.com/articles/single-seaters/f1/how
-much-does-an-f1-car-cost/?v=6cc98ba2045f.

Elson, James. "Top of the Flops: When F1 Failed in America." *MotorSport
Magazine*. October 14, 2023. https://www.motorsportmagazine.com/articles
/single-seaters/f1/top-of-the-flops-when-f1-failed-in-america.

Encyclopedia Britannica. "Automobile Racing." January 1, 2024. https://www
.britannica.com/sports/automobile-racing.

Encyclopedia Britannica. "Jack Brabham." May 15, 2024. https://www.britannica
.com/biography/Jack-Brabham.

ESPN8. "2019 Jelle's Marble Runs as Part of the Ocho." Accessed February 11,
2024. https://www.espn.com/watch/player/player?id=3815253.

ESPN. "A Beginner's Guide to F1 Terms and Tech." Accessed January 13, 2024.
https://www.espn.com/espn/feature/story/_/id/36180474/f1-terms-explained.

ESPN. "Osella." Accessed February 11, 2024. http://en.espn.co.uk/osella
/motorsport/team/411.html.

ESPN. "VTB Russian Grand Prix." Accessed February 10, 2024. https://www
.espn.com/f1/race/_/id/600014143.

ESPN UK. "The Shortest F1 Career of All Time." Accessed December 30, 2023.
http://en.espn.co.uk/onthisday/motorsport/story/2271.html#.

Eurosport. "Bianchi Crash Impact Was 254G." July 23, 2015. https://www
.eurosport.com/formula-1/bianchi-crash-impact-was-254g_sto4831070/story
.shtml.

F1 Chronicle. "The History of Formula 1 Safety Devices." January 8, 2021.
https://f1chronicle.com/the-history-of-formula-1-safety-devices-f1-history.

F1 Chronicle. "Which Formula 1 Track Is the Longest?" January 26, 2023.
https://f1chronicle.com/which-formula-1-track-is-the-longest.

F1 Experiences. "F1 Glossary: A–Z of the Most Commonly Used Terminology."
March 5, 2021. https://f1experiences.com/blog/f1-glossary-a-z-most-commonly
-used-terminology..

F1 Experiences. "RANKED: Top 10 Classic F1 Circuits to Experience in 2023."
November 21, 2022. https://f1experiences.com/blog/ranked-top-10-classic-f1
-circuits-to-experience.

The F1 Friend. "What Is F1 Silly Season?" August 7, 2022. https://www.f1friend
.com/blog/what-is-f1-silly-season?format=amp.

F1 Technical. "F1 Race Calendar 1950." Accessed February 9, 2024. https://www
.f1technical.net/f1db/events/index.php?year=1950.

Fearnley, Paul. "Mike Hawthorn: Britain's Forgotten World Champion."
MotorSport Magazine. February 2019. https://www.motorsportmagazine.com
/archive/article/february-2019/42/mike-hawthorn-britains-forgotten-world
-champion.

Ferrari. "Scuderia Ferrari History—1973." Accessed February 11, 2024.
  https://www.ferrari.com/en-EN/formula1/year-1973.

Ferrari. "Scuderia Ferrari History—1974." Accessed February 11, 2024.
  https://www.ferrari.com/en-EN/formula1/year-1974.

FIA. "2024 Formula 1 Sporting Regulations.—Issue 1." September 26, 2023.
  https://www.fia.com/sites/default/files/fia_2024_formula_1_sporting
  regulations-_issue_1_-_2023-09-26.pdf.

FIA. "2024 Formula 1 Technical Regulations—Issue 3." December 6, 2023.
  https://www.fia.com/sites/default/files/fia_2024_formula_1_technical
  regulations-_issue_3_-_2023-12-06.pdf.

FIA. "2023 Formula 1 Technical Regulations—Issue 4." December 7, 2022.
  https://www.fia.com/sites/default/files/fia_2023_formula_1_technical_regula-
  tions_-_issue_4_-_2022-12-07.pdf.

FIA. "2023 Formula 1 Sporting Regulations—Issue 8." December 6, 2023.
  https://www.fia.com/sites/default/files/fia_2023_formula_1_sporting
  regulations-_issue_8_-_2023-12-06_0.pdf.

FIA. "Auto+Medical—Safety in Our HANS." April 11, 2019. https://www.fia.com
  /news/auto-medical-safety-our-hans.

FIA. "Circuits Layout and Information." Accessed January 11, 2024.
  https://www.fia.com/sites/default/files/fia_circuit_list_template_2019.pdf.

FIA. "FIA Formula 2." Accessed February 4, 2024. https://www.fia.com/events
  /formula-2-championship/season-2023/fia-formula-2.

FIA. "FIA Formula 3." Accessed February 4, 2024. https://www.fia.com/events
  /fia-formula-3-championship/season-2023/fia-formula-3-0.

FIA. "Formula 4 Certified by FIA." Accessed February 4, 2024. https://www.fia
  .com/events/formula-4-certified-fia/season-2020/formula-4-certified-fia.

FIA. "Formula Regional Championships Certified by FIA." Accessed February 4,
  2024. https://www.fia.com/events/formula-regional-championships-certified-fia
  /season-2022/formula-regional-championships.

FIA. "List of Licensed FIA Circuits." Accessed January 11, 2024. https://www.fia
  .com/sites/default/files/circuits_fia20231022.pdf.

FIA. "Mohammed BEN SULAYEM: FIA President." 2022. https://www.fia.com
  /profile/mohammed-ben-sulayem.

FIA. "Organisation." Accessed August 8, 2023. https://www.fia.com/organisation.

Fiber Brokers International, LLC. "All About Zylon." Accessed September 9, 2023.
  https://fiberbrokers.com/technical-materials-recycling/all-about-zylon.

FKP. "Barriers." Accessed February 12, 2024. https://fkp-uk.com/tecpro-barrier.

Formula 1. "130R, Blanchimont and the Wall of Champions—Our Writers on the
  Trickiest Corners in Formula 1 History." June 16, 2022. https://www.formula1
  .com/en/latest/article/130r-blanchimont-and-the-wall-of-champions-our
  -writers-on-the-trickiest.2FDbAXxaAHdkjkTkZQeIby.

Formula 1. "2023 FIA Formula One World Championship." Accessed February 6,
  2024. https://www.formula1.com/en/racing/2023.html.

Formula 1. "Abu Dhabi 2023." Accessed February 6, 2024. https://www.formula1
  .com/en/racing/2023/United_Arab_Emirates/Circuit.html.

Formula 1. "Australia 2023." Accessed February 6, 2024. https://www.formula1
.com/en/racing/2023/Australia/Circuit.html.

Formula 1. "Austria 2023." Accessed February 6, 2024. https://www.formula1
.com/en/racing/2023/Austria/Circuit.html.

Formula 1. "Azerbaijan 2023." Accessed February 6, 2024. https://www.formula1
.com/en/racing/2023/Azerbaijan/Circuit.html.

Formula 1. "Bahrain 2023." Accessed February 6, 2024. https://www.formula1
.com/en/racing/2023/Bahrain/Circuit.html.

Formula1. "Bahrain to Name First Corner after Schumacher." March 2, 2014.
https://www.formula1.com/en/latest/headlines/2014/3/Bahrain-to-name-first
-corner-after-Schumacher.html.

Formula 1. "Belgium 2023." Accessed February 6, 2024. https://www.formula1
.com/en/racing/2023/Belgium/Circuit.html.

Formula 1. "Brazil 2023." Accessed February 6, 2024. https://www.formula1.com
/en/racing/2023/Brazil/Circuit.html.

Formula 1. "Canada 2023." Accessed February 6, 2024. https://www.formula1
.com/en/racing/2023/Canada/Circuit.html.

Formula 1. "China 2024." Accessed February 6, 2024. https://www.formula1.com
/en/racing/2024/China/Circuit.html.

Formula 1. "Drivers, Teams, Cars, Circuits and More—Everything You Need to
Know about Formula 1." Accessed February 5, 2024. https://amp.formula1.com
/en/latest/article.drivers-teams-cars-circuits-and-more-everything-you-need-to
-know-about.7iQfL3Rivf1comzdqV5jwc.html.

Formula 1: Drive to Survive. Seasons 1–5. Aired March 8, 2019 through February
24, 2023, Netflix.

Formula1. "Eau Rouge or Raidillon? Spa's 'Confusing' Corner Names." August 23,
2018. https://www.formula1.com/en/video/eau-rouge-or-raidillon-spas-confusing
-corner-names.6060945853001.

Formula 1. "F1 Academy Announces the Five Teams Entering 2023–2025
Seasons." December 16, 2022. https://www.formula1.com/en/latest/article
.f1-academy-announces-the-five-teams-entering-2023-2025-seasons
.23Bz3PQR8SslZbVET5zE7R.html.

Formula 1. "F1 Broadcast Information." Accessed January 14, 2024.
https://www.formula1.com/en/toolbar/broadcast-information.html.

Formula 1. "F1 Explained: How Does the Super License System Work—And
What Does Sargeant Need to Do to Qualify?" November 16, 2022.
https://www.formula1.com/en/latest/article.f1-explained-how-does-the-super
-licence-system-work-and-what-does-sargeant.IXyLbO00195LXtCo3YlOU.html.

Formula 1. "F1 Fantasy." Accessed September 30, 2023. https://fantasy.formula1
.com/en.

Formula1. "F1 Glossary." Accessed August 7, 2023. https://www.formula1.com
/en/championship/inside-f1/glossary.html.

Formula 1. "F1 Schedule 2024." Accessed February 6, 2024. https://www
.formula1.com/en/racing/2024.html.

Formula 1. "F1 Teams 2024." Accessed February 2, 2024. https://www.formula1
.com/en/teams.html.

Formula 1. "Fernando Alonso to Make Sensational Return to F1 with Renault in 2021." July 8, 2020. https://amp.formula1.com/en/latest/article .fernando-alonso-to-make-sensational-return-to-f1-with-renault-in-2021.70HoQC ymKlEllDzHFXkaBB.html.

Formula 1. "Formula 1 Statement on the Russian Grand Prix." February 25, 2022. https://www.formula1.com/en/latest/article.formula-1-statement -on-the-russian-grand-prix.4S39V28GpAH5ESb8LksW0J.html.

Formula1. "From Cutting Curfews to Grid Penalties—10 Rule Changes You Need to Know About for the 2023 F1 Season." Accessed January 15, 2024. https:// www.formula1.com/en/latest/article.from-cutting-curfews-to-grid-penalties -10-rule-changes-you-need-to-know.5EN5ENd23oOqFDnw8fD0rp.html?click ref=1100lyaBm7TN&dclid=CPfUjdGE34MDFZ_nlAkd0ZcKAg.

Formula 1. "Great Britain 2023." Accessed February 6, 2024. https://www .formula1.com/en/racing/2023/Great_Britain/Circuit.html.

Formula 1. "Hall of Fame: Alain Prost." Accessed January 3, 2024. https://www .formula1.com/en/drivers/hall-of-fame/Alain_Prost.html.

Formula 1. "Hall of Fame: Alan Jones." Accessed January 3, 2024. https://www .formula1.com/en/drivers/hall-of-fame/Alan_Jones.html.

Formula 1. "Hall of Fame: Alberto Ascari." Accessed January 3, 2024. https://www.formula1.com/en/drivers/hall-of-fame/Alberto_Ascari.html.

Formula 1. "Hall of Fame: Ayrton Senna." Accessed January 3, 2024. https://www.formula1.com/en/drivers/hall-of-fame/Ayrton_Senna.html.

Formula 1. "Hall of Fame: Damon Hill." Accessed January 3, 2024. https://www .formula1.com/en/drivers/hall-of-fame/Damon_Hill.html.

Formula 1. "Hall of Fame: Denny Hulme." Accessed January 3, 2024. https://www.formula1.com/en/drivers/hall-of-fame/Denny_Hulme.html.

Formula 1. "Hall of Fame: Emerson Fittipaldi." Accessed January 3, 2024. https://www.formula1.com/en/drivers/hall-of-fame/Emerson_Fittipaldi.html.

Formula 1. "Hall of Fame: Fernando Alonso." Accessed January 3, 2024. https://www.formula1.com/en/drivers/hall-of-fame/Fernando_Alonso.html.

Formula 1. "Hall of Fame: Graham Hill." Accessed January 8, 2024. https://www.formula1.com/en/drivers/hall-of-fame/Graham_Hill.html.

Formula 1. "Hall of Fame: Jack Brabham." Accessed January 8, 2024. https://www.formula1.com/en/drivers/hall-of-fame/Jack_Brabham.html.

Formula 1. "Hall of Fame: Jackie Stewart." Accessed January 3, 2024. https://www.formula1.com/en/drivers/hall-of-fame/Jackie_Stewart.html.

Formula 1. "Hall of Fame: Jacques Villeneuve." Accessed January 3, 2024. https://www.formula1.com/en/drivers/hall-of-fame/Jacques_Villeneuve.html.

Formula 1. "Hall of Fame: James Hunt." Accessed January 3, 2024. https://www.formula1.com/en/drivers/hall-of-fame/James_Hunt.html.

Formula 1. "Hall of Fame: Jenson Button." Accessed January 3, 2024. https://www.formula1.com/en/drivers/hall-of-fame/Jenson_Button.html.

Formula 1. "Hall of Fame: Jim Clark." Accessed September 10, 2023. https://www.formula1.com/en/drivers/hall-of-fame/Jim_Clark.html.

Formula 1. "Hall of Fame: Jochen Rindt." Accessed January 3, 2024. https://www.formula1.com/en/drivers/hall-of-fame/Jochen_Rindt.html.

Formula 1. "Hall of Fame: Jody Scheckter." Accessed January 3, 2024.
https://www.formula1.com/en/drivers/hall-of-fame/Jody_Scheckter.html.
Formula 1. "Hall of Fame: John Surtees." Accessed January 10, 2024.
https://www.formula1.com/en/drivers/hall-of-fame/John_Surtees.html.
Formula 1. "Hall of Fame: Juan Manuel Fangio." Accessed January 3, 2024.
https://www.formula1.com/en/drivers/hall-of-fame/Juan_Manuel_Fangio.html.
Formula 1. "Hall of Fame: Keke Rosberg." Accessed January 3, 2024.
https://www.formula1.com/en/drivers/hall-of-fame/Keke_Rosberg.html.
Formula 1. "Hall of Fame: Kimi Raikkonen." Accessed January 3, 2024.
https://www.formula1.com/en/drivers/hall-of-fame/Kimi_Raikkonen.html.
Formula 1. "Hall of Fame: Lewis Hamilton." Accessed January 26, 2024.
https://www.formula1.com/en/drivers/hall-of-fame/Lewis_Hamilton.html.
Formula 1. "Hall of Fame: Mario Andretti." Accessed January 3, 2024.
https://www.formula1.com/en/drivers/hall-of-fame/Mario_Andretti.html.
Formula 1. "Hall of Fame: Max Verstappen." Accessed January 3, 2024.
https://www.formula1.com/en/drivers/hall-of-fame/Max_Verstappen.html.
Formula 1. "Hall of Fame: Michael Schumacher." Accessed January 3, 2024.
https://www.formula1.com/en/drivers/hall-of-fame/Michael_Schumacher.html.
Formula 1. "Hall of Fame: Mika Hakkinen." Accessed January 3, 2024.
https://www.formula1.com/en/drivers/hall-of-fame/Mika_Hakkinen.html.
Formula 1. "Hall of Fame: Mike Hawthorn." Accessed January 8, 2024.
https://www.formula1.com/en/drivers/hall-of-fame/Mike_Hawthorn.html.
Formula 1. "Hall of Fame: Nelson Piquet." Accessed January 3, 2024.
https://www.formula1.com/en/drivers/hall-of-fame/Nelson_Piquet.html.
Formula 1. "Hall of Fame: Nico Rosberg." Accessed January 3, 2024.
https://www.formula1.com/en/drivers/hall-of-fame/Nico_Rosberg.html.
Formula 1. "Hall of Fame: Nigel Mansell." Accessed January 3, 2024.
https://www.formula1.com/en/drivers/hall-of-fame/Nigel_Mansell.html.
Formula 1. "Hall of Fame: Niki Lauda." Accessed January 3, 2024.
https://www.formula1.com/en/drivers/hall-of-fame/Niki_Lauda.html.
Formula 1. "Hall of Fame: Nino Farina.html." Accessed January 2, 2024.
https://www.formula1.com/en/drivers/hall-of-fame/Nino_Farina.html.
Formula 1. "Hall of Fame: Phil Hill." Accessed January 8, 2024. https://www
.formula1.com/en/drivers/hall-of-fame/Phil_Hill.html.
Formula 1. "Hall of Fame: Sebastian Vettel." Accessed January 3, 2024.
https://www.formula1.com/en/drivers/hall-of-fame/Sebastian_Vettel.html.
Formula1. "'He Was Like a Ghost'—Remembering Niki Lauda's Comeback from
Fiery Nurburgring Crash, 45 Years On." July 28, 2021. https://amp.formula1
.com/en/latest/article.he-was-like-a-ghost-remembering-niki-laudas-comeback
-from-fiery-nurburgring.5YAP47xm3tGb3Vp5pdakX.html.
Formula 1. "Horner Explains Why Red Bull Opted to Partner with Ford Instead of
'Incredible Company' Honda for 2026." February 3, 2023. https://www
.formula1.com/en/latest/article/horner-explains-why-red-bull-opted-to-partner
-with-ford-instead-of.4TxWiQTxtwg8gjSZlZR9j8.
Formula 1. "Hungary 2023." Accessed February 6, 2024. https://www.formula1
.com/en/racing/2023/Hungary/Circuit.html.

Formula 1. "'Inspirational' Hamilton Included on TIME 100 List of Most Influential People in 2020." September 23, 2020. https://amp.formula1.com/en/latest/article.inspirational-hamilton-included-on-time-100-list-of-most-influential-people.iCnRW3CngLjB5S4Qi4ehZ.html.

Formula 1. "Italy 2023—01–03 Sep." Accessed February 6, 2024. https://www.formula1.com/en/racing/2023/Italy/Circuit.html.

Formula 1. "Italy 2023—19–21 May." Accessed February 6, 2024. https://www.formula1.com/en/racing/2023/EmiliaRomagna/Circuit.html.

Formula 1. "Italy—Monza." Accessed February 5, 2024. https://www.formula1.com/en/information.italy-autodromo-nazionale-monza.FiJN1jnQIRLeHqOxlt13m.html.

Formula 1. "Japan 2023." Accessed February 6, 2024. https://www.formula1.com/en/racing/2023/Japan/Circuit.html.

Formula 1. "Logan Sargeant." Accessed February 11, 2024. https://www.formula1.com/en/drivers/logan-sargeant.html.

Formula 1. "Maria Teresa de Filippis, First Female F1 Racer, Dies at 89." January 9, 2016. https://www.formula1.com/en/latest/headlines/2016/1/maria-teresa-de-filippis--first-female-f1-racer--dies-at-89.html.

Formula 1. "Mexico City 2023." Accessed February 6, 2024. https://www.formula1.com/en/racing/2023/Mexico/Circuit.html.

Formula 1. "Mexico Names Final Corner after Nigel Mansell." September 15, 2015. https://www.formula1.com/en/latest/headlines/2015/9/mexico-names-final-corner-after-nigel-mansell.html.

Formula 1. "Monaco 2023." Accessed February 6, 2024. https://www.formula1.com/en/racing/2023/Monaco/Circuit.html.

Formula 1. "Netherlands 2023." Accessed February 6, 2024. https://www.formula1.com/en/racing/2023/Netherlands/Circuit.html.

Formula 1. "Qatar 2023." Accessed February 6, 2024. https://www.formula1.com/en/racing/2023/Qatar/Circuit.html.

Formula 1. "Saudia Arabia 2023." Accessed February 6, 2024. https://www.formula1.com/en/racing/2023/Saudi_Arabia/Circuit.html.

Formula 1. "Senior Management." Accessed January 26, 2024. https://corp.formula1.com/team.

Formula 1. "Silverstone Circuit." Accessed February 5, 2024. https://www.formula1.com/en/racing/2023/Great_Britain/Circuit.html.

Formula 1. "Singapore 2023." Accessed February 6, 2024. https://www.formula1.com/en/racing/2023/Singapore/Circuit.html.

Formula 1. "Spain 2023." Accessed February 6, 2024. https://www.formula1.com/en/racing/2023/Spain/Circuit.html.

Formula 1. "Strange but True: F1's Weirdest and Most Amazing Records." August 16, 2016. https://www.formula1.com/en/latest/features/2016/8/strange-but-true--f1-s-weirdest-and-most-amazing-records.html.

Formula1. "Stream F1 Live, Your Way." January 14, 2024. https://www.formula1.com/en-us/subscribe-to-f1-tv.

Formula 1. "United States 2023—05–07 May." Accessed February 6, 2024. https://www.formula1.com/en/racing/2023/Miami/Circuit.html.

Formula 1. "United States 2023—16–18 Nov." Accessed February 6, 2024.
https://www.formula1.com/en/racing/2023/Las_Vegas/Circuit.html.

Formula 1. "United States 2023—20–22 Oct." Accessed February 6, 2024.
https://www.formula1.com/en/racing/2023/United_States/Circuit.html.

Formula 1. "WATCH: The Origins of Ground Effect." April 5, 2022. https://www
.formula1.com/en/latest/article.watch-the-origins-of-ground-effect.6i1MZBs5xe
6cjO2deb57hV.html.

Formula 1. "What's in a Name? The History behind Silverstone's Iconic Corners."
July 3, 2015. https://www.formula1.com/en/latest/features/2015/7/what_s-in-a
-name--the-history-behind-silverstones-iconic-corners.html.

Formula 1. "Williams—Year by Year." Accessed February 11, 2024. https://www
.formula1.com/en/teams/Williams/Year_by_Year.html.

Fox Sports. Reiman, Samuel. "Tragedy at Spa: The 1960 Belgian Grand Prix."
June 19, 2017. https://www.foxsports.com/stories/motor/tragedy-at-spa-the
-1960-belgian-grand-prix.

Galloway, James. "Red Bull Crash Pair Reprimanded." Sky Sports. December 11,
2018. https://www.skysports.com/f1/news/12433/11352821/max-verstappen
-daniel-ricciardo-reprimanded-for-all-red-bull-azerbaijan-gp-crash.

George, Dhruv. "WATCH: Jean Alesi Sent Flying after Collision with Ferrari Driver
Eddie Irvine." Essentially Sports. June 30, 2020. https://www.essentiallysports
.com/f1-news-watch-jean-alesi-sent-flying-after-collision-with-ferrari-driver-eddie
-irvine.

Gilboy, James. "Why Some People Think Lotus Founder Colin Chapman Faked
His Death." The Drive. March 21, 2022. https://www.thedrive.com/news
/44570/why-some-people-think-lotus-founder-colin-chapman-faked-his
-death.

Glenn. "RIP the Lollipop Man." Formula One Art & Genius. October 12, 2013.
https://www.f1-grandprix.com/?p=39809.

Goldia, Cep. "Gallery: The Evolution of a Formula 1 Car Since 1950." Motorsport.
com. March 28, 2017. https://us.motorsport.com/f1/news/gallery-the
-evolution-of-a-formula-1-car-since-1950-887292/3020200/#gal-3020200-m0
-jim-clark-lotus-25-climax-11614106.

Goodhart, Benjie. "Le Mans 1955: The Disaster That Changed Motorsport
Forever." June 11, 2020. GQ. https://www.gq-magazine.co.uk/lifestyle/article
/le-mans-1955-disaster.

Goodley, Alvin. "9 Most Expensive Sports in the World." Rarest.org. December 9,
2022. https://rarest.org/sports/expensive-sports.

Gran Turismo. 2023. IMDb. Accessed February 12, 2024. https://www.imdb.com
/title/tt4495098.

The Guardian. "FIA President Defends Sexist Remarks and Denies 'Inhuman'
Misogyny Claims." November 28, 2023. https://www.theguardian.com
/sport/2023/nov/28/fia-president-mohammed-ben-sulayem-defends-sexist
-remarks-denies-misogyny-claims-f1.

Gupta, Manas Sen. "5 Places in the World Where You Can Drive a Formula 1 Car
Like A Pro." Lifestyle Asia. March 27, 2022. https://www.lifestyleasia.com/ind
/tech/auto/places-to-drive-a-formula-1-car/amp.

Habib, Hal. "'58 Cuban Grand Prix: Death, Gangsters, A Revolution and Champion Driver Fangio Kidnapped." *The Palm Beach Post*. April 21, 2023. https://www.palmbeachpost.com/story/sports/2023/04/21/castros-kidnapping -of-juan-manuel-fangio-fit-plot-of-1958-cuban-grand-prix/70082038007.

Haldenby, Nicky. "Every Italian Circuit which Formula 1 Has Visited." F1 Destinations. May 16, 2023. https://f1destinations.com/every-italian-f1-circuit.

Hanson, Gareth. "Turbo Tech 101—What Is a Turbo Wastegate and How Does It Work?" AET Turbos. December 2, 2014. https://aet-turbos.co.uk/turbo-tech-101 -what-is-a-turbo-wastegate-and-how-does-it-work.

Hardy, Ed. "F1 Prize Money: How Much Teams Will Earn after the 2023 Season." Autosport. December 10, 2023. https://www.autosport.com/f1/news/f1-prize -money-how-much-teams-will-earn-after-the-2023-season/10550469.

Hardy, Ed. "F1 Records Broken by Max Verstappen in 2023." Autosport. January 2, 2024. https://www.autosport.com/f1/news/f1-records-broken-by-max -verstappen-in-2023/10543882.

Hardy, Ed. "How Long Is an F1 Race? Laps, Time, Distance, and More Explained." Motorsport.com. February 5, 2024. https://www.motorsport.com /f1/news/how-long-is-an-f1-race-laps-time-distance-explained/10554259.

Harrington, Alex. "What's the Difference Between F1 Constructor Standings and Driver Standings?" *Sports Illustrated*. March 2, 2023. https://www.si.com /fannation/racing/f1briefings/track-guides/whats-the-difference-between-f1 -constructor-standings-and-driver-standings.

Hawley, Dustin. "What Is the Average Horsepower of a Car?" J.D. Power. December 11, 2022. https://www.jdpower.com/cars/shopping-guides/what-is -the-average-horsepower-of-a-car.

Holding, Joe. "What Do Drs, Black and White Flag, Porpoising, and More Mean? F1 Terms Explained." Auto Sport. April 22, 2022. https://www.autosport.com /f1/news/f1-terms-explained-what-box-marbles-drs-undercut-and-more -mean-5477591/5477591.

Holt, Sarah. "The Master Chefs Who Fuel F1." CNN. July 24, 2014. https://edition .cnn.com/2014/07/24/sport/motorsport/f1-master-chefs-motorsport/index.html.

Holthouse, Richard, dir. 2011. *Midsomer Murders*, Season 14, Episode 1, "Death in the Slow Lane." Aired March 23, 2011, on ITV.

Horn, Gerhard. "Take a Taxi Ride in Red Bull's Two-Seater F1 Car." CarBuzz. August 15, 2022. https://carbuzz.com/news/take-a-taxi-ride-red-bulls-two-seater -f1-car.

Horncastle, Rowan. "Classified of the Week: A Three-Seat F1 Car." Top Gear. April 6, 2017. https://www.topgear.com/car-news/classified-week-three-seat-f1-car.

Horner, Scott. "Here Are the Key Differences between F1 and IndyCar." IndyStar. March 23, 2023.

Howard, Ron, director. 2013. *Rush*. Working Title Films.

Hughes, Mark. 2023. "Playing Catch-up." MotorSport, December 2023.

Hughes, Mark and Giorgio Piola. "Tech Tuesday: The Lotus 79, F1's Ground Effect Marvel." Formula 1. February 15, 2022. https://www.formula1.com/en/latest /article.tech-tuesday-the-lotus-79-f1s-ground-effect-marvel.sAD9PXt7mC 8iMSwwe6CCw.html.

Hughes, Mark. "Ricciardo and Verstappen's Explosive Baku Crash: Team-Mate Battle That Shaped Red Bull." MotorSport. May 3, 2023. https://www .motorsportmagazine.com/articles/single-seaters/f1/ricciardo-and-verstappens -explosive-baku-crash-team-mate-battle-that-shaped-red-bull.

Hunt, Ben. "DADS & LADS F1's 14 Father and Son Duos as Michael Schumacher's Son Mick Becomes Latest, Following Verstappen, Hill, and Rosberg." *The Sun*. March 27, 2021. https://www.thesun.co.uk/sport/14442057 /f1-famous-father-son-duos-schumacher/amp.

Hunt, Scott. "The Forgotten Story of … Jochen Rindt." *The Guardian*. March 3, 2015. https://amp.theguardian.com/sport/blog/2015/mar/03/formula-one-motor -sport-jochen-rindt-scott-hunt.

HyperRacer. "Aspendale Park Speedway: The World's First Purpose Built Car Racing Track—Australia 1905." Accessed January 13, 2024. https://www .hyperracer.com/history.

Indianapolis Motor Speedway. "Indianapolis 500 Historical Stats—Race Results—Indianapolis 500—1955." Accessed January 15, 2024. https://www .indianapolismotorspeedway.com/events/indy500/history/historical-stats/race -stats/race-results/1955.

Indianapolis Motor Speedway. "Indianapolis 500 Historical Stats—Race Results—Indianapolis 500—1958." Accessed January 15, 2024. https://www .indianapolismotorspeedway.com/events/indy500/history/historical-stats/race -stats/race-results/1958.

Indy Speedway. "Fatalities—May 1953." Accessed May 27, 2024. https://indy motorspeedway.com/memorial_1953.html.

Instagram. "Roscoe Hamilton." Accessed January 27, 2023.https://www.ins-tagram.com/roscoelovescoco?igsh=andiaDI3YjF5YTA=.

Irimia, Silvian. "Story of the Legendary Brabham BT46B Fan Car and Some Forgotten Facts About It." Autoevolution. January 7, 2023. https://www .autoevolution.com/news/story-of-the-legendary-brabham-bt46b-fan-car-and -some-forgotten-facts-about-it-207631.html.

Jaiswal, Samriddhi. "F1 Out Lap: What Is the Difference Between an Out Lap and In Lap?" The Sports Rush. March 19, 2022. https://thesportsrush.com /f1-news-f1-out-lap-what-does-out-lap-means-in-formula-1.

Jeffries, Tom. "The 10 Best Formula 1 Drivers Ever: Hamilton, Schumacher & More." Autosport. July 30, 2023. https://www.autosport.com /f1/news/whos-the-best-formula-1-driver-schumacher-hamilton -senna-more-4983210/4983210.

Jogia, Saajan. "F1 News: Lewis Hamilton Drops Big Clue on Brad Pitt Formula One Movie Release." *Sports Illustrated*. December 20, 2023. https://www .si.com/fannation/racing/f1briefings/news/f1-news-lewis-hamilton-drops -big-clue-on-brad-pitt-f1-movie-release-time-sj4.

Jogia, Saajan. "F1 News: Ralf Schumacher's Emotional Update on Brother Michael Schumacher." *Sports Illustrated*. November 4, 2023. https://www .si.com/fannation/racing/f1briefings/news/f1-news-ralf-schumachers-emotional -update-on-brother-michael-schumacher-sj4.

Johnson, Todd. "How Is Carbon Fiber Made?" ThoughtCo. January 13, 2020. https://www.thoughtco.com/how-is-carbon-fiber-made-820391.

Jolly, Jasper and Giles Richards. "From F1 Supremo to Tax Fraud Conviction: The Rise and Fall of Bernie Ecclestone." *The Guardian.* October 12, 2023. https://www.theguardian.com/sport/2023/oct/12/rise-and-fall-of-bernie -ecclestone-formula-one.

Jones, Bruce. 2023. *Formula One: The Illustrated History.* Devon: Leaf Publishing LTD.

Joseph, Sam. "Logan Sargeant Becomes the First American to Score a Formula One Point in 30 years." CNN. October 23, 2023. https://www.cnn.com/2023/10/23 /sport/logan-sargeant-f1-american-grand-prix-spt-intl/index.html.

Kapur, Sahil. "America's Only Formula 1 Driver Is fighting for His Future. He Says He Knows 'Exactly' What He Needs to Do." NBC News. October 20, 2023. https://www.nbcnews.com/news/sports/americas-only-formula-one-driver -fighting-future-says-knows-exactly-ne-rcna121275.

Kershaw, Emma. "Geri Halliwell-Horner and Christian Horner: All About Their Relationship." *People.* December 25, 2023. https://people.com /all-about-geri-halliwell-horner-christian-horner-relationship-8400151.

Kew, Matt. "F1 Pauses South African GP Plans for 2024." Motorsports.com. June 6, 2023. https://us.motorsport.com/f1/news/f1-pauses-south-african-gp -plans-for-2024/10479405.

Kew, Ollie. "Top Gear's Top 9: Formula One Game-Changers." TopGear. Accessed January 1, 2024. https://www.topgear.com/car-news/motorsport/top-gears-top -9-formula-one-game-changers.

King, Alanis. "Nepotism Wins." Jalopnik. November 30, 2018. https://jalopnik .com/nepotism-wins-1830766974.

King, Alanis and Elizabeth Blackstock. "What You Find When You Look Into Rich Energy, the Mystery Sponsor of America's F1 Team." Jalopnik. Accessed December 30, 2023. https://jalopnik.com/what-you-find-when-you-look-into -rich-energy-the-myste-1833303620.

Kohli, Charanjot Singh. "Top 5 Youngest F1 World Champions." Sportskeeda. August 11, 2023. https://www.sportskeeda.com/f1/top-5-youngest-f1-world -champions.

Kristensen, Stefan. "What Does 'Delta Positive' Mean In Formula 1?" Motorsport Explained. January 28, 2022. https://motorsportexplained.com/f1-delta-time.

Kristensen, Stefan. "What's the Difference Between F1, F2, F3, F4, and FE?" Motorsport Explained. December 25, 2021. https://motorsportexplained.com /difference-between-f1-f2-f3-f4-and-fe.

Las Vegas Weekly. "Anatomy of a Formula 1 Race Car." November 16, 2023. https://lasvegasweekly.com/news/2023/nov/16/anatomy-of-a-formula-1-race-car.

Leeuwen, Andrew van. "Three-Seater F1 Car to Make Adelaide Appearance." Motorsport.com. January 4, 2023. https://us.motorsport.com/f1/news/three -seater-f1-car-adelaide-appearance/10416882.

Liberty Media Corporation. Liberty Media. "Liberty Media Corporation Completes Acquisition of Formula 1." January 23, 2017. https://www.libertymedia.com /news/detail/305/liberty-media-corporation-completes-acquisition-of-formula-1.

Lillibury, Simon. "How Silverstone's Rich History Links World War Two and a Dead Sheep." The Sportsman. July 11, 2019. https://www.thesportsman.com /articles/how-silverstone-s-rich-history-links-world-war-two-and-a-dead-sheep.

Lusson, Damien. "Formula 1 Car Weight | Everything You Need to Know." Motorsport.com. September 1, 2023. https://las-motorsport.com/f1/blog /formula-1-car-weight-everything-you-need-to-know/5046/#:~:text=The%20 FIA%20establishes%20a%20minimum,lbs)%20for%20the%202023%20 season.

Lynch, Steven. "The Unexplained Mystery of 'Taffy' von Trips." ESPN. June 4, 2010. http://en.espn.co.uk/f1/motorsport/story/19236.html.

Maher, Thomas. "What Are F1 Teams Permitted to Do with Their Cars on 'Filming Day' Shakedowns?" Planet F1. February 1, 2023. https://www.planetf1.com /news/what-are-f1-filming-day-shakedowns-rules.

McFerran, Damian. "FLASHBACK—The Day Sega Took Over an F1 Race, and Ayrton Senna Lifted a Sonic Trophy." Time Extension. March 21, 2023. https://www.timeextension.com/features/flashback-the-day-sega-took-over -an-f1-race-and-ayrton-senna-lifted-a-sonic-trophy.

Melissen, Woulter. "The 'Last Truly Independent F1 Team' Exits." Revs Institute. Accessed February 11, 2024. https://automedia.revsinstitute.org/the-last-truly -independent-f1-team-exits.

Merriam-Webster.com Dictionary. Definition of "chicane." Accessed February 10, 2024. https://www.merriam-webster.com/dictionary/chicane.

Mercedes AMG F1. "F1 Explained: Everything You Need to Know about Wind Tunnels." Accessed January 28, 2024. Educational video, 3:16. https://www .mercedesamgf1.com/news/f1-explained-1.

Merriam-Webster.com Dictionary. Definition of "silly season." Accessed February 7, 2024. https://www.merriam-webster.com/dictionary/silly%20season.

Midsomer Murders Season 14, Episode 1: "Death in the Slow Lane." IMDB. Accessed September 17, 2023. https://www.imdb.com/title/tt1722764.

Miles, Ben. "F1's Five Biggest Fails." Goodwood Motorsport. June 16, 2020. https://www.goodwood.com/grr/f1/f1s-five-biggest-fails.

Miles, Ben. "The Nine Greatest F1 Controversies." Goodwood Motorsport. September 14, 2020. https://www.goodwood.com/grr/f1/the-nine-greatest-f1 -controversies.

Miller, Caleb. "Formula E's Gen3 Car Is Faster, Lighter, and More Efficient." Car and Driver. April 29, 2022. https://www.caranddriver.com/news/a39861521 /formula-e-gen3-revealed/#.

Mishra, Abhinandan. "Influential Lobby in U.K. Resisting Mallya's Extradition to India." *The Sunday Guardian*. January 22, 2023. https://sundayguardianlive .com/news/influential-lobby-uk-resisting-mallyas-extradition-india.

Mitchell, Rory. "Video: How an F1 Drinks System Works." RacingNews 365. January 30, 2023. https://racingnews365.com/video-how-an-f1-drinks-system -works.

Mitchell, Scott. "Robert Kubica Says He Had Signed F1 Deal with Ferrari for 2012." Autosport. July 11, 2018. https://www.autosport.com/f1/news/robert -kubica-says-he-had-signed-f1-deal-with-ferrari-for-2012-5297347/5297347.

The Mob Museum. "NASCAR Rooted in Prohibition Bootlegging." Accessed February 3, 2024. https://prohibition.themobmuseum.org/the-history/prohibition-potpourri/nascar-and-prohibition.

Mohan, Ashwath. "Hypercar vs Formula 1 Car: Are the Cars Used at Le Mans Faster?" SportsManor. June 14, 2023. https://sportsmanor.com/f1-hypercar-vs-formula-1-car-are-the-cars-used-at-le-mans-faster.

MotorSport. "Can Hamilton Save Ferrari? The F1 Drivers Who Tried to Change the Scuderia." February 1, 2024. https://www.motorsportmagazine.com/articles/single-seaters/f1/can-hamilton-save-ferrari-the-f1-drivers-who-tried-to-change-the-scuderia.

MotorSport. "Max Verstappen's F1 Records—The Ones He Beat and Broke in 2023." November 26, 2023. Updated November 27, 2023. https://www.motorsportmagazine.com/articles/single-seaters/f1/max-verstappens-f1-records-and-the-ones-he-can-still-break-in-2023.

Motorsport.com. "Alonso Does It Again with Bahrain GP Win." April 5, 2005. https://us.motorsport.com/f1/news/alonso-does-it-again-with-bahrain-gp-win/1214619.

Motorsport.com. "Insider's Guide: Rules of Overtaking." March 29, 2022. https://us.motorsport.com/f1/news/insiders-guide-rules-of-overtaking/7427185.

Motorsport.com. "Insider's Guide: Who Does What in an F1 Team?" Last updated February 19, 2023. https://us.motorsport.com/f1/news/insiders-guide-f1-team-who-does-what/8025043.

Motorsport.com. "Insider's Guide: Why do F1 Regulations Change?" February 19, 2023. https://us.motorsport.com/f1/news/why-do-f1-regulations-change/7827958.

Motorsport.com. "Jann Mardenborough and Red Bull Racing." Last updated February 17, 2014. https://www.motorsport.com/f1/news/jann-mardenborough-and-red-bull-racing/3220014.

Motorsport.com. Malsher-Lopez, David. "Why Sir Stirling Moss was 'Mr. Motor Racing.'" April 12, 2021. https://www.motorsport.com/f1/news/stirling-moss-mr-motor-racing/4779795.

Motorsport.com. "My Job in Racing: F1 Scrutineering." January 10, 2018. https://us.motorsport.com/f1/news/my-job-in-racing-f1-scrutineer-992835/1386152.

Motorsports Hall of Fame. "Peter Revson." Accessed February 12, 2024. https://www.mshf.com/hall-of-fame/inductees/peter-revson.html.

Motorsport Tickets. "How Many Laps Does Each Formula 1 Race Have?" June 30, 2021. https://motorsporttickets.com/blog/how-many-laps-does-each-formula-1-race-have.

Motorsport Tickets. "Formula 1 Records: Most Wins, Pole Positions and World Championships." November 20, 2023. https://motorsporttickets.com/blog/formula-1-records-most-wins-pole-positions-and-world-championships.

Motortrend. "Aerodynamics in Race Cars Explained—Aspects of Race Car Aerodynamics—Ultimate Racing." Accessed February 2, 2024. https://www.motortrend.com/how-to/ctrp-0908-aerodynamics-in-race-cars-explained/amp

Mulder, Nicole. "What Will Change in Formula 1 in 2024?" *GP Blog*. December 21, 2023. https://www.gpblog.com/en/news/253929/what-will-change-in -formula-1-in-2024.html.

Næss, Hans Erik. "'In Case of Dispute, the French Text is to be Used': A History of the Association Internationale des Automobile Clubs Reconnus (AIACR), 1904–1922." The International Journal of the History of Sport. November 30, 2023. https://www.tandfonline.com/doi/full/10.1080/09523367.2023.2286332.

Nair, Sanket. "What Is a Practice Start in F1?" Essentially Sports. June 28, 2021. https://www.essentiallysports.com/f1-news-what-is-a-practice-start-in-f1.

National Motor Museum. "Chitty Chitty Bang Bang." Accessed January 13, 2024. https://nationalmotormuseum.org.uk/vehicle-collection/chitty-chitty-bang-bang.

National Museum Australia. "Jack Brabham Wins First World Championship." Accessed May 26, 2024. https://www.nma.gov.au/defining-moments /resources/jack-brabham-wins-first-world-championship.

Newey, Adrian. 2017. *How to Build a Car*. Read by Richard Trinder. New York: Harper Collins. Audible audio ed., 12 hr., 26 min.

New York Times. "Rindt, 28, Is Killed in Crash at Monza." September 6, 1970. https://www.nytimes.com/1970/09/06/archives/rindt-28-is-killed-in-crash-at -monza-rindt-dies-as-car-crashes-in.html.

New York Times. "Two Die in a Crash At Denmark Trials; British Racer Killed." July 30, 1967. https://timesmachine.nytimes.com/timesmachine/1967/07/31 /90384087.pdf?pdf_redirect=true&ip=0.

Nguyen, Christian and Ben Nigh. "How NASCAR banked turns help keep drivers safe and faster." Business Insider. May 16, 2021. https://www.businessinsider .com/nascar-banked-turns-help-drivers-safe-faster-race-cars-2019-7#.

Noble, Jonathan. "Formula One Racing for Dummies Cheat Sheet." For Dummies. October 5, 2023. https://www.dummies.com/article/home -auto-hobbies/sports-recreation/auto-racing/formula-one-racing-for-dummies -cheat-sheet-300781.

Noble, Jonathan. *Formula One Racing for Dummies—2nd Edition*. Hoboken, NJ: For Dummies, 2023.

Noble, Jonathan. "Red Bull Reveals Ricciardo's Tyres Trapped at Back of Garage." Motorsport.com. May 29, 2016. https://www.motorsport.com/f1/news/red-bull -reveals-ricciardo-s-tyres-trapped-at-back-of-garage-741863/741863.

Noble, Jonathan and Mark Hughes. *Formula One Racing for Dummies*. Hoboken, NJ: For Dummies, 2003.

Noble, Jonathan and Mark Hughes. "Formula One Racing: What Happens During an F1 Pit Stop." For Dummies. June 23, 2022. https://www.dummies.com /article/home-auto-hobbies/sports-recreation/auto-racing/formula-one-racing -what-happens-during-an-f1-pit-stop-201586.

Nunez, Alex. "That Time Star Wars Took Over Red Bull Racing." *Road and Track*. November 28, 2014. https://www.roadandtrack.com/car-culture/entertainment /g5749/photos-star-wars-red-bull-racing-f1-takeover-in-2005.

Opong, Rich. "What Is An F1 Super Licence? (And the Path to Getting One)." FlowRacers. June 23, 2022. https://flowracers.com/blog/what-is-an-f1-super -licence.

Parkes, Ian. "A Stunning Comeback for Fernando Alonso in Formula 1." *New York Times.* May 18, 2023. https://www.nytimes.com/2023/05/18/sports/autoracing /f1-fernando-alonso.html.

Petric, Darjan. "2005 Japaense GP—Raikkonen Beats Fisichella to Win from 17th on the Grid." Max F1. September 10, 2020. https://maxf1.net/en/2005 -japanese-gp-raikkonen-beats-fisichella-to-win-from-17th-on-the-grid.

Piola, Giorgio. "The McLaren That Changed Formula 1 History." Motorsport.com. April 12, 2021. https://us.motorsport.com/f1/news/the-car-that-changed -formula-1-history.

Piola, Giorgio and Matthew Somerfield. "The Rise and Fall of Bargeboards in F1." Autosport. February 3, 2022. https://www.autosport.com/f1/news/rise-and-fall -of-bargeboards-in-f1/7239198.

Pirelli. "F1 Tyres." Accessed January 29, 2024. https://www.pirelli.com/tyres/en -ww/motorsport/f1/tyres.

Piscoti, Tyler. "The Gran Turismo Movie Tells a Remarkable True Story-With One Big Exception." Biography. Last updated December 18, 2023. https://www .biography.com/movies-tv/a44796145/gran-turismo-movie-true-story-jann -mardenborough.

PlanetF1. "Revealed: 10 Crazy F1 Records That Will Never Be Broken Again." December 23, 2023. https://www.planetf1.com/features/10-crazy-f1-records -unbeaten.

Pretorius, Louis. "Do F1 Drivers Keep Their Trophies?" One Stop Racing. January 8, 2022. https://onestopracing.com/do-f1-drivers-keep-their-trophies.

ProTech Composites. "The Past, the Present, and the Future of Carbon Fiber." Accessed September 9, 2023. https://protechcomposites.com/news/the-past -the-present-and-the-future-of-carbon-fiber.

Prydderch, Hannah. "2023 F1 Academy Grid: Introducing the Drivers and Teams for the All-Female Series' Inaugural Season." Formula 1. April 7, 2023. https://www.formula1.com/en/latest/article.2023-f1-academy-grid-introducing -the-drivers-and-teams-for-the-all-female.7CtUAdswc3i5pU4yVJ08XH.html.

Pryson, Mike. "Celebrating Nico Hulkenberg: The 20 F1 Drivers with the Most Career Starts without a Win." Autoweek. Last updated October 27, 2023. https://www.autoweek.com/racing/formula-1/g32792184/most-career-f1-starts -without-win.

Radu, Vlad. "Lotus 25: The Legendary Race Car That Changed Formula 1 Forever." Autoevolution. August 9, 2023. https://www.autoevolution.com/news/lotus-25 -the-legendary-race-car-that-changed-formula-1-forever-219267.html.

Reardon, Logan. "How Much Are F1 Drivers Paid? Here Are the Salaries for Every Driver in 2023." NBC Miami. November 16, 2023. https://www .nbcmiami.com/news/sports/how-much-are-f1-drivers-paid-here-are-the -salaries-for-every-driver-in-2023/3160911.

Reuters. "Timeline: The 2011 Uprising in Bahrain and What's Happened Since." February 16, 2021. https://www.reuters.com/article/idUSKBN2AG1K6.

Red Bull. Verolme, Harry. "Everything you Need to Know about F1 Sprint Weekends in 2023." October 24, 2023. https://www.redbull.com/us-en/2023 -f1-sprint-format-everything-you-need-to-know.

Red Bull Racing. "Red Bull's Guide To: The Pit Wall." July 30, 2020. https://www .redbullracing.com/int-en/bulls-guide-to-the-pit-wall.

Red Bull Ring. "Red Bull Ring History." Accessed February 9, 2024. https://www .redbullring.com/en/history.

Reilly, Luke. "Pole Model: How Namco's Pole Position Revolutionised Racing." IGN. December 19, 2022. https://www.ign.com/articles/pole-model-how -namcos-pole-position-revolutionised-racing.

Richard Morris Racing. "Biography." Accessed February 11, 2024. https://richardmorrisracing.com/biography.

Richard Morris Racing. "Proud to Be a Driver Ambassador for Racing Pride." Accessed February 11, 2024. https://richardmorrisracing.com/racing-pride.

Richards, Giles. "'Cash Is King': Lewis Hamilton Criticises Australian GP Green Light Amid Covid-19." *The Guardian*. March 12, 2020. https://amp.theguardian .com/sport/2020/mar/12/two-more-haas-team-members-tested-for-covid-19 -on-eve-of-australian-grand-prix.

Rimmer, Lucy. "How Much Does an F1 Car Weigh in 2023 and What's Included in the Limit?" Motorsport.com. June 15, 2023. https://us.motorsport.com/f1 /news/how-much-does-an-f1-car-weigh-in-2023/10437686/#:~:text=The%20 original%20limit%20was%20set,electronic%20items%20in%20the%20car.

RN 365. "Engine F1." Accessed February 4, 2024. https://racingnews365.com /engine-f1.

RN 365. "McLaren Boss Brown Reveals His New Tattoo!" October 24, 2021. https://racingnews365.com/brown-reveals-his-new-tattoo.

RN 365. "Women in Formula 1." Accessed January 15, 2024. https://racingnews 365.com/woman-in-f1.

Roarington. "Colin Chapman and Lotus—A Disappearance as Fast as His Cars." April 23, 2021. https://roarington.com/media-house/stories/colin-chapman-and -lotus4-a-disappearance-as-fast-as-his-cars.

Rookie Road. "Which Formula 1 Races Are Held At Night?" Last updated February 14, 2023. https://www.rookieroad.com/formula-1/which-formula -one-races-are-held-at-night-5576425.

Roy, Abhranil. "Best F1 Rivalries | Top 5 greatest rivalries in the Formula 1." Chase Your Sport. December 22, 2020. https://www.chaseyoursport.com/Formula-1 /Top-5-biggest-rivalries-in-the-Formula-1/2205.

Rush (2013). IMDb. Accessed September 10, 2023. https://www.imdb.com/title /tt1979320/?ref_=ext_shr_lnk.

S., Paulius. "A Legend Who Revolutionized Formula One—Colin Chapman." March 21, 2022. https://dyler.com/blog/38/a-legend-who-revolutionized-formula -one-colin-chapman.

Saha, Debarati. "Everything You Need to Know About F1 Helmet Visors and How They Work in the Rain." November 18, 2020. Essentially Sports. https://www .essentiallysports.com/f1-news-everything-you-need-to-know-about-f1-helmet -visors-and-how-they-work-in-the-rain.

Saha, Debarati. "Why Do F1 Drivers Train Their Necks?" Essentially Sports. December 27, 2020. https://www.essentiallysports.com/why-do-f1-drivers-train -their-necks.

Saunders, Nate. "The Bizarre Haas-Rich Energy Saga Explained." ESPN. March 3, 2020. https://www.espn.com/f1/story/_/id/27221746/the-bizarre-haas-rich -energy-saga-explained.

Saunders, Nate. "Red Bull Handed $7 Million Fine, 10% Wind-Tunnel Reduction for Budget-Cap Breach." ESPN. October 28, 2022. https://www.espn.com/f1 /story/_/id/34895717/red-bull-handed-7-million-fine-10-percent-windtunnel -reduction-budget-cap-breach.

Schwartz, Nick. "Fernando Alonso Says Goodbye to Formula 1 in Emotional Video." *USA Today*. August 14, 2018. https://ftw.usatoday.com/2018/08 /fernando-alonso-says-goodbye-to-formula-1-in-emotional-video.

Seymour, Mike. "The Beginner's Guide to… Formula 1 Tyres." Formula 1. April 9, 2023. https://amp.formula1.com/en/latest/article.the-beginners-guide-to -formula-1-tyres.61SvF0Kfg29UR2SPhakDqd.html.

Seymour, Mike. "Everything You Need to Know about F1's Newest Circuit in Madrid—Including What Makes It So Unique." Formula 1. January 23, 2024. https://www.formula1.com/en/latest/article.everything-you-need-to-know -about-f1s-newest-circuit-in-madrid-including.I6oJZDAE9HVa4Ge8LZOZA.html.

Shanahan, Paul. "Whitianga Festival of Speed 2010 another Roaring Success." Sailworld Cruising. May 12, 2010. https://www.sailworldcruising.com/n /Whitianga-Festival-of-Speed-2010-another-Roaring-Success/-69420.

Skybrary. "Bernoulli's Principle." Accessed January 28, 2024. https://skybrary .aero/articles/bernoullis-principle.

Sky Sports. "The Dictionary: Your F1 A to Z." February 12, 2016. https://www .skysports.com/f1/news/9945329/the-f1-dictionary-everything-you-need-to -know-from-a-to-z.

Sky Sports. "The Red Bulls Collide!" December 11, 2018. https://www.skysports .com/f1/news/12433/11351903/azerbaijan-gp-max-verstappen-and-daniel -ricciardos-red-bulls-collide.

Silvestro, Brian. "F1 Teams Have the Strangest History." *Road and Track*. February 11, 2009. https://www.roadandtrack.com/motorsports/a26293139/f1-team -history-explainer-video.

Siregar, Aditya. "Worst moments Ferrari has had from the 1950s after entering F1." Motorsport.com. September 21, 2017. https://us.motorsport.com/f1/news /worst-moments-ferrari-has-had-from-the-1950s-after-entering-f1 -955825/3047627.

Smedley, Rob. "Testing Explained: Rob Smedley on Flow-Vis Paint." Formula 1. February 21, 2019. https://amp.formula1.com/en/latest/article.testing-explained -rob-smedley-on-flow-vis.7nU2VePGlVrhIGa8wgCoLE.html.

Smith, Fred. "Here's How Mercedes-AMG F1's Dual-Axis Steering Worked." *Road and Track*. December 14, 2020. https://www.roadandtrack.com/news /a34962680/mercedes-amg-f1-dual-axis-steering-explained.

Smith, Fred. "12 Years after Near-Fatal Crash, F1 Hero Robert Kubica Signs with Ferrari." *Road and Track*. November 22, 2023. https://www.roadandtrack.com/news/a45918936/robert-kubica-signs-ferrari-12-years-after-crash.

Smith, Luke. "Inside the Piranha Club, the Ruthless World of F1 Politics." The Athletic. February 28, 2023. https://theathletic.com/4258479/2023/02/28/formula-1-politics-piranha-club/?amp=1.

Smith, Richard. "Secrets of Underbody Tunnels, Rear Diffusers and Venturis." Symscape. April 24, 2007. https://www.symscape.com/blog/secrets_of_diffusers.

Somerfield, Matt and Giorgio Piola. "Uncovered: The First Tech Tricks Exposed at F1 2023 Testing." Motorsport.com. February 24, 2023. https://www.motorsport.com/f1/news/f1-tech-secrets-test-2023-cars/10435707.

The Sound of Speed. 1962. IMDb. Accessed February 12, 2024. https://www.imdb.com/title/tt0405334/?ref_=fn_al_tt_1.

Sports Illustrated. "Every Sportsperson of the Year." Last updated December 6, 2022. https://www.si.com/sports-illustrated/2018/12/10/sportsman-year-covers#gid=ci0254f57580082580&pid=2022.

Srinivasan, Hiranmayi. "Here's How F1 Teams and Drivers Make Millions." Investopedia. Last updated July 5, 2023. https://www.investopedia.com/the-economics-of-formula-1-here-s-how-f1-teams-and-drivers-make-millions-7555800.

Srinivasan, Hiranmayi. "Rob McElhenney Is Investing in Formula 1 Team, Alpine—Here's McElhenney's Net Worth." Investopedia. June 28, 2023. https://www.investopedia.com/rob-mcelhenney-is-investing-in-formula-1-team-alpine-here-s-mcelhenney-s-net-worth-7554786.

Stab. "The Genesis of the Shoey… with the Mad Huey's Hazza Twins." November 26, 2016. https://stabmag.com/news/the-genesis-of-the-shoey-with-the-mad-hueys-hazza-twins.

Steer, Fiona. "Give It 107%—What Is 107% Rule in F1?" *The Sun*. March 21, 2023. https://www.thesun.co.uk/sport/21784150/what-is-the-107-rule-in-f1/amp.

Straw, Edd. "Analysis: The Historical Impact of F1's New Double Points Rule." Autosport. December 10, 2013. https://www.autosport.com/f1/news/analysis-the-historical-impact-of-f1s-new-double-points-rule-4469783/4469783.

Straw, Edd. 2023. "Viva Las Vegas?" MotorSport, December 2023.Straw, Edd. "Why has F1's silly season been pushed back to 2025?" Racer. January 29, 2024. https://racer.com/2024/01/29/why-has-f1s-silly-season-been-pushed-back-to-2025.

Stuart, Greg. "A Beginner's Guide to… F1 Slang." Formula 1. February 8, 2020. https://www.formula1.com/en/latest/article.a-beginners-guide-to-f1-slang.1Pg6tvGZ2y7u4KAnc8WXGl.html.

Stuart, Greg. "Unlucky for some—13 of F1's Most Unfortunate Records." Formula 1. February 6, 2021. https://www.formula1.com/en/latest/article.unlucky-for-some-13-of-f1s-most-unfortunate-records.2MgJsNRazBTqQdZdoVuWZM.html.

"Styling: McLaren MP4-98T 2 Seater Concept." Andy Blackmore Design. Accessed February 5, 2024. http://www.andyblackmoredesign.com/portfolio /mclaren-mp4-98t-2-seater-concept.

The Sunday Times. "What Is F1 Halo, When Was It Introduced, and How Does It Save Lives?" July 5, 2022. https://www.driving.co.uk/news/motor-sport/f1 -halo-explained.

Sutherland, Ben. "F1 in Africa: How Team Gunston Started a Sponsorship Revolution." BBC Sport. March 6, 2023. https://www.bbc.com/sport/africa /64684013.amp.

Sylt, Christian. "The $400 Million Loss That Put the Brakes on F1's Force India Team." *Forbes.* October 8, 2018. https://www.forbes.com/sites/csylt /2018/10/08/the-400-million-loss-that-put-the-brakes-on-f1s-force-india-team /amp.

Szymkowski, Sean. "Here's What Every Button on an F1 Steering Wheel Does." Motor Authority. March 23, 2019. https://www.motorauthority.com /news/1122204_heres-what-every-button-on-an-f1-steering-wheel-does.

Tomlinson, Sam. "Racing Royalty: Wolfgang 'Taffy' Von Trips." Paddock Legends. March 23, 2020. https://www.paddock-legends.com/en/news/racing-royalty -wolfgang-taffy-von-trips-2020-03-23/b-215/?t=218.

Topgear Autoguide. "F1 Rules from 1950 to Today: The Eleven Eras of Formula 1." February 4, 2019. https://topgear-autoguide.com/category/formula-1/f1-rules -from-1950-to-today-the-eleven-eras-of-formula-11607790862.

Tremayne, David. "OBITUARY: Tony Brooks, Formula 1's Racing Dentist, Remembered." Formula 1. May 3, 2022. https://www.formula1.com/en/latest /article.obituary-tony-brooks-formula-1s-racing-dentist-remembered.25Cx3o gmFmnkoNgZXADjm4.html.

Tremayne, David. "Trailblazing Racer Lella Lombardi Remembered, 30 Years from Her Death." Formula 1. March 3, 2022. https://www.formula1.com/en/latest /article.trailblazing-racer-lella-lombardi-remembered-30-years-on-from-her-dea th.6zz9pupcxc97yy5SEL1kkR.html.

Tripathi, Gunaditya. "Why Does Daniel Ricciardo Perform the Shoey Celebration on the Podium?" Sportskeeda. April 19, 2023. https://www.sportskeeda.com /f1/why-daniel-ricciardo-perform-shoey-celebration-podium.

Tromans, Phill. "F1 Vs IndyCar: The Differences Explained." CarThrottle. August 14, 2023. https://www.carthrottle.com/news/f1-vs-indycar-differences -explained.

Untitled Formula One Racing Movie. 2024. IMDb. Accessed February 12, 2024. https://www.imdb.com/title/tt16311594/?ref_=fn_al_tt_1.

USA Today (Associated Press). "Lewis Hamilton Receives Knighthood Days after Losing Formula One Title." December 15, 2021. https://www.usatoday.com /story/sports/motor/formula1/2021/12/15/lewis-hamilton-formula-one -receives-knighthood-after-losing-title/8909476002.

Vaughn, Mark. "1958 Portuguese Grand Prix Tells You All You Need to Know about Stirling Moss." Autoweek. April 13, 2020. https://www.autoweek.com/racing /formula-1/a32121966/stirling-moss-at-the-1958-portuguese-grand-prix.

Vogan, Travis. 2018. "Appendix 2: ABC's Wide World of Sports Athlete of the Year." *ABC Sports*. Oakland: University of California Press. https://doi.org/10.1525/9780520966260-013.

Waddell, Adam. "Formula One: Here Are the Family Trees of Every Team." Top Gear. Accessed August 15, 2023. https://www.topgear.com/car-news/formula-one/formula-one-here-are-family-trees-every-team.

Walker, Kate. "For Fernando Alonso, a Career of Victories." *New York Times*. June 15, 2019. https://www.nytimes.com/2019/06/15/sports/autoracing/fernando-alonso-victories-timeline.html.

Wallace, Bubba. "The 100 Most Influential People of 2020—Lewis Hamilton." *Time*. September 22, 2020. https://time.com/collection/100-most-influential-people-2020/5888433/lewis-hamilton.

Walthert, Matthew. "Monaco Grand Prix: How Each Corner of the Famous Circuit De Monaco Got Its Name." Bleacher Report. May 21, 2014. https://bleacherreport.com/articles/2071604-monaco-grand-prix-how-each-corner-of-the-famous-circuit-de-monaco-got-its-name.

Wecker, Janaya. "Rules You Didn't Know Formula 1 Drivers Have to Follow." *Popular Mechanics*. Updated February 28, 2023. https://www.popularmechanics.com/adventure/sports/g39527552/formula-1-driver-rules.

Weeks, Jim. "The Death of Ayrton Senna and the Long Search for Blame." Vice. April 28, 2017. https://www.vice.com/en/article/4xjj4n/death-ayrton-senna-and-the-search-for-blame-williams-imola-san-marino-adrian-newey.

Westbrook, Justin T. "Here's How Virtual Safety Cars Work in Formula One." Jalopnik. March 5, 2023. https://jalopnik.com/heres-how-virtual-safety-cars-work-1826237975.

Whiley, Mark. "Queen Was 'Wonderful Driver' Who Wouldn't Let F1 Champion Jackie Stewart behind the Wheel." Daily Star. September 13, 2022. https://www.dailystar.co.uk/sport/f1/queen-sir-jackie-stewart-f1-27981412.

Williams, Ashley. "Experts Explain the Science behind Formula One Cars." News@TheU. May 5, 2022. https://news.miami.edu/stories/2022/05/experts-explain-the-science-behind-formula-one-cars.html.

Williams, Richard. "Tony Brooks Obituary." *The Guardian*. May 4, 2022. https://www.theguardian.com/sport/2022/may/04/tony-brooks-obituary.

Williamson, Martin. "Crashgate Explained." ESPN. Accessed September 18, 2023. http://en.espn.co.uk/f1/motorsport/story/14272.html.

Williamson, Martin. "Deaths in Formula One." Accessed January 15, 2024. http://en.espn.co.uk/f1/motorsport/story/3838.html.

Williamson, Martin. "A Timeline of Formula One." Accessed July 29, 2023. http://en.espn.co.uk/f1/motorsport/story/3836.html.

Wilson, Trevor. "What Is Dyno Testing?" Fabreeka. October 31, 2022. https://blog.fabreeka.com/what-is-dyno-testing.

Woodhouse, Jamie. "Ex-Force India owner Mallya sentenced to jail." PlanetF1. July 12, 2022. https://www.planetf1.com/news/vijay-mallya-sentenced-jail.

Woodhouse, Jamie. "Lewis Hamilton Convinced Niki Lauda Didn't Like Him before He Signed for Mercedes." Planet F1. April 21, 2023. https://www.planetf1.com/news/lewis-hamilton-niki-lauda-relationship.

Woodyatt, Amy. "Why Was This Weekend's F1 Title So Controversial?" CNN. December 13, 2021. https://www.cnn.com/2021/12/13/motorsport/f1 -hamilton-verstappen-controversy-intl-scli-spt/index.html.

Youson, Matt. "Imola '94 and the Lasting Safety Legacy." Formula 1. May 2, 2019. https://www.formula1.com/en/latest/article.imola-94-and-the-legacy-of -improved-safety.5P8zqEzNjKzYw8qdckoYFF.html.

YouTube. "Coronavirus VII: Sports: Last Week Tonight with John Oliver (HBO)." May 18, 2020. https://www.youtube.com/watch?v=z4gBMw64aqk.

YouTube. "Jelle's Marble Runs—Videos." Accessed February 11, 2024. https://www.youtube.com/@JellesMarbleRuns.

YouTube. "Kimi Raikkonen's Greatest-Ever Drive through the Field | 2005 Japanese Grand Prix." December 7, 2021. https://www.youtube.com/watch ?v=zf4axwL-jPU.

YouTube. "Martin Brundle's EPIC Albert Park Shunt in 1996." F1 Australian Grand Prix. March 22, 2023. https://www.youtube.com/watch?v=3MmZbbevTi8.

The Zolo Blog. "The Most Expensive Sports Ever." November 17, 2023. https://zolostays.com/blog/the-most-expensive-sports-ever.

ACKNOWLEDGMENTS

I'd like to acknowledge all the people past, present, and future who have and do work tirelessly to make Formula 1 and all its racing siblings happen, and those who have strived to make the sport safer and safer for participants and crowds alike over the years.

A huge thanks to my parents and teachers for feeding my curiosity so that I never tire of broadening my horizons and learning new things.

Many thanks (and sometimes apologies) to everyone at Ulysses Press who toiled to made this book happen and fixed my sometimes ill-chosen words, including but not limited to Claire Sielaff, Yesenia Garcia-Lopez, Renee Rutledge, Claire Chun, and Mary Calvez.

And thanks, love, and hugs to Jeff for supporting me through all of my projects despite my many unhealthy writing habits.

Best to all! And see you at the races.

ABOUT THE AUTHOR

Bernadette "Berni" Johnson began her career at age six, when she crayoned a book about her mom that received a rave review from its lone reader. On a bit of a trivia kick, her recent works include *The Big Book of Spy Trivia*, *The Big Book of Horse Trivia for Kids*, and *The Big Book of Cryptid Trivia*. When she's not watching movies or fiddling with a computer, she studies history, science, and other fun stuff, reads and writes fiction and nonfiction, and does the bidding of her terror of a terrier. You can read Berni's blog and find links to her writing at BerniJohnson.com.